# SPOILS
## OF
# WAR

# SPOILS
# OF
# WAR

Charles J. Levy

Houghton Mifflin Company Boston

1974

# Contents

# Introduction

THIS BOOK HAD its origins in a working class Irish neighborhood of Boston where the young men going off to war took
great pride in their patriotism. With the frequency of a cliché,
they claimed their neighborhood had the highest enlistment
rate in the country. But after returning from Vietnam, their
pride had turned to fear. For they now had a capacity for uncontrolled violence that resulted from their combat experiences.
In a group of sixty randomly selected Marine veterans, two
were indicted for murders and five for attempted murders during one year.

Even before the veterans returned home, it was clear that
their neighborhood could not be described as nonviolent.
Nevertheless, their fights had previously been controlled by
elaborate and carefully observed rules that limited the level of
violence. Boundaries around time and space were inoperative
now, for the veterans believed they were in Vietnam while com-
mitting their violence. Additional boundaries, such as the one
between friend and enemy, were also war casualties. Their
victims were likely to be relatives or fellow members of a
group.

I observed, and to some extent shared, the lives of these
veterans at their homes, taverns and street corners. This ex-
ploration was part of a study that I conducted during a three

year period in the Department of Psychiatry at the Harvard Medical School. The project initially involved the sixty Marine veterans. In order to determine whether their pattern of violence was peculiar to marines, sixty Army veterans from the same neighborhood were added to the study. It turned out that all members of both groups experienced these psychological returns from Vietnam with varying degrees of violence.

It was still unknown whether this violence was peculiar to Vietnam veterans living in this particular neighborhood. An answer was provided as a result of testifying before the United States Senate's Subcommittee on Veterans' Affairs about the need for a Federal program to assist veterans in readjusting to civilian life. It led to requests for assistance from veterans, their families or lawyers. These veterans were from every type of background in all parts of the country. In most cases, they had been charged with or convicted of murder.

Although this book focuses on one type of readjustment problem, the discussion about it is relevant to other problems. For instance, drugs are not specifically covered. But many combatants considered them a means of coping with the frustrations of a guerrilla war that are described here. In addition, many veterans considered drugs a means of coping with the frustrations of returning home that are described here (or, if they became addicted in Vietnam, they used drugs at home without being able to consider them).

Nor is deliberate violence against others covered. But for the veteran there is often only a thin line separating it from uncontrolled violence against others and deliberate violence against himself. This was the case with a veteran who observes, "I'm not back from 'Nam when I think about it sometimes. I have my ghost and my feelings of terror." He had experiences in Vietnam and later at home that were similar to many of those in the following narratives. As an example, "You hate yourself and you want death." He was referring to his own

death and to the reason for his joining De Mau Mau — an
organization in Chicago that is comprised of blacks waging
war against whites. He deliberately instructed the membership
in the techniques of combat that he had learned, mostly
from the Viet Cong. Yet the murder he was convicted of occurred at a time when he believed himself to be in Vietnam.
Accordingly, he reported the killing to a policeman whom he
thought was his commanding officer.

Because Vietnam provides veterans with a frame of reference, it is the starting point for this book. It was only to make
the material more manageable that Chapters I and III are concerned with marines from the Boston neighborhood. Their
Vietnam and civilian experiences were interchangeable with
the ones reported by the Army veterans. This interchangeability has made it possible to combine veterans from both
branches in the fourth chapter. Later chapters are based
on my interviews with a cross-section of the veterans in other
parts of the country (including one veteran of the War who
was still in the Army). The narratives in all chapters are taken
from transcripts of tape recordings which were edited only to
the extent of removing my questions.

Perhaps a more helpful starting point for the book would
have been a description of the veterans' American experience
that preceded their Vietnam experience. This included a belief in the invincibility of technology. But the constraints of a
guerrilla war demonstrated the limits of technology. The Boston veterans discovered these limits as did a veteran who grew
up in a rural area at the opposite end of the United States. He
is not one of those presented later in this book, but he could
easily be. During his first combat operation in Vietnam he
found himself in a column of tanks and armored personnel car-
riers that was more advantageous to the Viet Cong than it was
to the Army: "Can you imagine the noise of sixteen tracked
vehicles? For sure, there aren't any surprise attacks on the

enemy. Usually, they're waiting and well dug in." After traveling a half mile, the lead tank hit a mine that the Viet Cong made out of an American artillery shell. The other vehicles then formed a "herring bone":

> Every vehicle turned at an angle to his left or right opposite to the vehicle in front of him. A couple of platoons of grunts of The Big Red One were pulling a ground sweep in the thick bush on each side of us. With all the fire power the column was delivering we killed four of The Big Red One's men. They came out of the woodline carrying them. And you never saw such dagger looks in your life. I put the four men in bags and shortly after this the medevac chopper arrived. I loaded the four dead grunts. Total enemy body count: zero. But plenty of shot up trees and bushes. That night was one of many more I spent thinking and sleepless.

When he first climbed into one of these vehicles: "I felt superior, like no gook could ever get to me." On a later operation, the lead tank again hit a mine so that it blocked the road. The North Vietnam Army with its hand-held weapons was then able to "hit every tank in order. They were well set up and didn't miss one." In this part of his narrative he no longer speaks of "gooks." They are now "NVA."

Another, related, tenet of the American experience was also undermined by his Vietnam experience: "Winning is all I've ever been taught." Both in Vietnam and back home, which is now a state penitentiary, he has found it "very hard to get used to being a loser." The connection between losing in the guerrilla war and losing again in civilian life is what this book seeks to explore.

# SPOILS
## OF
# WAR

# CHAPTER I

# Stories about the War

A COMBAT VETERAN observed that "there are a lot of 'twenty-mile sniper typewriter jockies' who spent their entire tour there in secure areas like Saigon that boast of killing hundreds of VC and NVA. You can usually tell the Viet vet that saw action by the stories he doesn't tell." The following are stories he does not ordinarily tell. These narratives cannot be considered war stories in any traditional sense — any more than the War can be considered a traditional war. Instead of the bravado that has characterized war stories of the past, these are often more in the nature of confessions. Failures of every kind are described in place of triumphs. What is implicit in several accounts was made explicit by the veteran who described not only how a marine was killed by a Viet Cong booby trap, but also how the selection of a civilian as surrogate was, in retrospect, a deeper failure. At the deathwatch for the old man, ". . . we laughed. And human beings don't do things like that." He uses the first person, but also indicates his transformation from a person. This disengagement from themselves as warriors helps to explain why the veterans were telling stories about the war, instead of war stories. It is not so much that they are describing what they did in the War as what the War did to them.

## 1. *Marines and Village Men*

I was in Vietnam for about a week I guess. This is the first time I ever seen any combat or anything. I looked over into the rice paddies. And I seen this thing floating in the rice paddies. It looked like a nigger. And so I was kind of stunned.

And I said, "Jesus. There's somebody over there."

So I went running over with the lieutenant. And it was the staff sergeant. He was a white guy. But he looked like a nigger he had got blown so bad.

The lieutenant grabbed the sergeant and he says, "O.K. Lift him out of the paddy."

I reached under to lift him out of the paddy and my hand just went right into him. There was nothing but guts.

I rolled him over. And Jesus I was fucking really sick. And I didn't know what to do. I took out my cartridge belt 'cause half of his head was blown like. I put his head on it so he wouldn't drown in his own blood. The blood started dripping out.

I said, "What do we do now?"

So the lieutenant says, "I'll take care of him."

So I says, "O.K." 'Cause I was stunned.

He says, "Get over to my jeep. You sit and guard the stuff I've got in there."

I was walking over toward the jeep and I looked back. And I seen the lieutenant grab his head and twist it back over so that he would drown in his own blood.

And like it just fucked my whole mind up. And I stood there and I puked.

Then somebody said, "Get him. He's around here some place." It was a command detonated mine.

We ran into the vil. We knew that they seen where the guy run.

We said, "Where did he go?" We all had our rifles on them and shit.

And like everybody said, "We don't know where he is." And one of the guys opened up and just started blowing people away.

Then they said, "He's over there. He's over there." And some went running up there.

And the fucking lieutenant screamed to me and another guy. He says, "Get in the three-sixty. A helicopter is coming in."

So we got around in a fucking circle. And I guess the lieutenant seen that I was kind of fucked up. So he come over to me and he said, "What's the matter?"

I said, "What the fuck did you kill the guy for?" 'Cause that's what he did.

"Well you seen the condition he was in. His leg was blown off. His balls were blown off. One arm and half of his head," he said. "He wouldn't have lived anyhow. And I just couldn't see him suffering any longer."

So, you know, I understood it. But I really didn't understand it.

When we got back to the base camp they says "We're going to name the camp Camp A."

The guy's name was Staff Sergeant A. And seeing how I was the one that noticed him and shit and I was kind of fucked up still in the head, the lieutenant says, "You build the sign."

So we went out. And we were building a sign. It was a red sign with yellow print on it: Base Camp Staff Sergeant A. We were on a hill and I fucked up somehow on the sign. The sign was kind of slanted a little bit. I put one hole in deeper than the other.

Then this fucking sergeant, he worked in the office. He had never seen anybody get fucking shot in all the time he was in Vietnam. He come over to me and says, "What the fuck are you doing man?" He says, "Don't you realize a man died for that fucking sign? Fix that fucking sign right."

I said, "You motherfucker." I says, "I was the one that pulled him out of the rice paddy."

"I don't give a fuck," he said. "Don't you realize . . ."

And I picked up a .45 and I started blowing fucking holes through the sign. I got a fifteen dollar fine.

It just fucks up your head somehow. Like that same day when the mine went off an old man, he was about eighty years old, got hit in the head with a piece of the shrapnel. A gook.

When we come back after the mine sweep he was outside his hooch. And all his relatives and friends and everything were sitting around and crying and shit.

And we laughed.

And human beings don't do things like that. But we stayed there and we fucking laughed until he died.

So it turns you into some sort of fucking animal.

☆ ☆ ☆

This gook was coming in and the patrol was coming in.

The point told him to halt. But he starts to walk into the elephant grass. So they shot an M-79, this grenade launcher, at him. And that missed him or wounded him. He wasn't going to stop for nothing.

So finally he run across a clearing. And a marine sniper on top of the hill got him with three rounds. Fired three times into the side. Tore his body out. And then they brought him into the village.

The villagers come over to see if any of their relatives were hurt. The gook happened to be a member of the village. He also was mentally retarded. And that's why he ran. There was a lot of fucking people screaming, crying and shit.

And I asked the sniper, "Was he armed?"

He says, "How the fuck do I know? I ain't taking no chances with them."

Anyway, they got them out. He died, I guess, or something. It doesn't really matter. But I remember they were really upset about that.

And about a week later we got overrun. I think that the villagers knew that the VC were coming. And they didn't give us any kind of warning. They blew up two of our vehicles and shit and killed about five of us and wounded eight others.

We got this one son of a bitch that night. While he was lying there we all circled around him. He was calling for a doctor. So this gunnery sergeant with a scar, he was really an animal type, real fucking perfect marine. He gave him the coup de grâce.

And he said, "Anybody else want him?"

So everybody started shooting him. And the next morning we tied a rope to his leg, his good leg, and we tied this rope to a motorized mule. And we dragged him through the village. So all the fucking slopes could see it. We got out to the dump. We chopped the rope and left him out in the dump. And like later on the slopes come up and buried him.

It was sort of like a little lesson.

I forget the name of the place. It was just a sand plot. It was our artillery forward fire base is what it was. If they were my buddies got killed or something I'd know where I was.

But this was some fucking phony place between Chu Lai and Danang. And it was curfew out. At night gooks can't walk more than approximately fifty paces from their village. And they can't fuck around. They have to carry a torch at night if they move around. If they don't they can be shot. And if they move away from that village they can be shot.

There was three guys in the bunker and it was the most forward position in our perimeter. B was there sleeping. And the other two guys were awake. They were boots.

So they said, "Corporal B, Corporal B, some fucking body up there with a light."

You know, they were fucking really shook up about it. They were sort of like trigger-happy.

He says, "They can leave the village. They can walk fifty paces. He's probably just taking a shit."

They said, "Corporal B, he keeps on walking. He doesn't even look like he's going to stop."

He says, "Well if he walks another ten yards tell me." He didn't want to get up. And he started to sleep. And then the gook walked ten more meters.

They said, "He's still walking."

And B got up. And he had a machine gun in the bunk.

He went, "Where is he? Oh yeah."

And he started to judge the distance. At night it's tough to do that too because your depth perception is fucked up and stuff. And he's clearing all the shit out of his eyes, trying to judge how far away the gook is.

He says, "Hold your fucking finger out." He's going the old two-finger stuff trying to judge how far away.

"That should be ten meters, twenty meters." Then, "That fucking gook's fifty meters away."

He took the machine gun and placed it in the shoulder and leaned down and cocked it and released the safety and tracked him. And the two boots were getting a kick out of it. They didn't think he'd shoot him though.

B said, "One more fucking step and then I'll give it to him. If he don't turn around or stop."

And the gook walked. And he let him have it. He shot a hundred-round belt into that fucking slope. He just pumped rounds in. The whole belt he shot in there.

So the whole fucking place went on alert. And fucking flares went up. And everybody's opening up on whatever's scaring them that night. It gives you an excuse to let loose. The whole fucking place went crazy. All the fucking gooks in all the villages went into their little bunkers that they built for just such occasions. And finally they calmed it all down.

The next morning they had a patrol go outside and find him. Right at dawn. And it was easy to find 'cause he was out in these dried-up rice paddies.

And he was fucking shot to shit. All hundred rounds must have hit him. He was completely perforated. He looked like a fucking piece of cheese. And he was about ninety-nine years old too. He hadn't got a fucking thing on him, like military. Like grenade or any type of booby trap anywhere near him. And he's a village elder. That kind of thing.

It didn't do a hell of a lot for our public relations.

So he come back in and the shit started. We had a fucking battery formation. Everybody fell out.

And the gunny come out and blew his stack. He was pissed off 'cause we were tight with that village.

He said, "You know how old that fucking gook was you killed?"

☆  ☆  ☆

Like a farmer going by with a load of hay. I seen somebody drop a match in it.

☆  ☆  ☆

I remember one time with the gooks, it was an argument as to who was going to get our garbage. The local villagers had a beef with us because we had hired, sort of, an outside firm. We wouldn't pay them anything. But they would have the garbage. They had this little truck and it had like a fucking lawn mower engine. They used to sell the garbage. But the villagers want it for their own animals and like the meat they used to keep.

About four hundred meters away from the base was a garbage dump. And a road went out to it. And like we used to dump all our garbage out there in burners. So the village representatives said, "You just come out and throw it away. And we'll see what we can salvage out of it. Then we'll set it on fire." So we agreed to this.

We were coming in off a patrol. And we seen all the fucking gooks there. So we thought maybe somebody killed one of the villagers. And they was all complaining about it. And there was a fucking truck there. And the people were ready to rip the people in the truck apart. And the fucking sentries didn't know what was going on.

So they locked the gate. It could have been a terrorist move. And they could have thrown a grenade into the fucking place or rushed four or five fucking members of the sappper team in with machine guns and fucking shot the place up. We walked up there and they were all yelling and screaming. And there was a fucking spokesman.

So this fucking gunnery sergeant came out. He was arguing with the gooks. And they were saying that it was screwing them economically. And they didn't like it. But unfortunately the commanding officer had agreed to these other people.

It seemed like a logical thing to do but he hadn't taken into consideration the local villagers. One of these fucking punks happened to be a suspected communist and he was doing all the talking.

See, there was some gooks out on the wire one night. And they went into the village and they fucking shot a couple of people. And he come running up to the wire. He speaks fluent English. And he was yelling who he was. And the fucking guys at the sentry gate knew who he was. So they shone the spotlights on the fucking bum. And he was standing out there.

He says, "Don't shoot me." He says, "Fucking Ho Chi Minh."

So he told how he was captured but broke loose. And that fucker was the biggest liar in the world. They had to kill some people in the village. And they knew he was one of their sympathizers so they had to let him escape.

Anyway we dragged him in for interrogation. Then he was released, because they couldn't prove where his head was at. And he was doing all the fucking talking. The people were ready to riot. All we had to do was push them all out of the way and let the truck go in.

I thought the people in the local area should have forgot it. It was hot as hell. I was tired. We had been on patrol most of the morning. And I fucking didn't want to sit out there. And I was out of water too. Just had to sit there listening to the stupid fucking lifer that was running the patrol. Had us form some type of circle around the truck. It was laughable.

And we were sitting there looking at each other. Saying, "What the fuck is this?"

He said, "Fix bayonets!" So we all fucking fixed bayonets. And the people are watching us. And they backed off a little bit. And they were kind of worried. They didn't know what the fuck was going to happen at first. And then they seen looks on our faces. And we were as confused as they were about it. And they recognized that.

So they decided, "These fucking marines aren't going to stab us." They were right. We wouldn't have. But we would've hit them with the fucking butt of the rifle. They push the little kids in first. They know we'd never hurt them.

And they come running through. So you grab the little

fucking punk. And you throw him in the fucking dirt. Then they all rushed in. And they were fucking pulling the truck apart and shit and, oh, it was fucking funny.

Then the gunnery sergeant knew who the troublemaker was and walked over and fucking calmly punched the shit out of him. And that fucking kind of stopped it.

And then he said, "Take him prisoner."

We grabbed that fucking bum. Threw him on the fucking ground. Kicked him. Push out position. All the fucking people got fucking enraged. Then fucking everybody let the bolt go home. We did that for the effect. If you let the bolts go home it slows them down.

But these people were really fucking nuts. It's the first time I've ever seen fucking Vietnamese really get excited about their own fucking thing. They were getting mad. And we were getting mad. 'Cause the more they fucking argued with us, the more ridiculous it seemed that we had to put up with the fucking little God damn zipper-heads.

There was more fucking people coming down. And there was fucking troops waiting outside. Then nobody knew what the fuck was going to happen. We knew we weren't going to shoot them all. But the gooks weren't sure either.

And somebody fucking fired off a fucking pistol. And everybody stopped. There was a big hush.

And our interpreter was rushed out. And he was talking in Vietnamese. You ever hear fucking gooks arguing you wouldn't believe they could understand what they're saying.

Then he fucking shot at one of them. That did it. Everybody fucking stopped then. He didn't hit anyone. Shot at somebody's fucking feet. He yelled some more in the fucking mike. Pointed his pistol around. They all fucking screwed.

Then the village chief come in with some fucking elders. And they all sat around. And they brought some heavies from other villages in the area. And a representative from each hamlet of that village. All in their Sunday fucking best. The marine truck went out and picked them up. They all got in the back like important people. Brought them into the position. They all sat there. Very important fucking types.

The truck driver isn't fucking too impressed with any of them. They expected the gate to be opened for them and fucking somebody bring up some portable steps so they could get down on them. He said, "O.K., pile out." So they all got out. And they all stood around the fucking thing.

The CO, I guess, decided to fucking make them wait. And they finally fucking got the garbage. And they fucking all walked out. And they were very happy. They were all laughing and holding hands.

They all hold hands, see. I fucking hate that.

## 2. *Marines and Village Women*

There were a lot of times we would buzz by on jeeps.

And the broads would be riding bicycles. And we'd just roll by and hold them by the fucking cunt while we're driving. And they'd fucking squirm. They didn't want to fall off. And we'd be doing like two miles an hour, as fast as they were doing. And we'd just hold them and laugh at them and try to work your finger in there. And they'd be going fucking crazy. And swearing at you in Vietnamese. And you're laughing.

And then it depended on what kind of guy you are, if you fucking pushed them off into fucking rice paddies or let them go. They usually fall off. Or just jump off.

If they were a prostitute it sort of ruined it all. 'Cause they'd fucking smile and fucking say, "Follow me." You say, "Oh fuck it." And then you push her over.

We used to sneak broads in.

They used to come through the wire. They knew where each one of the booby traps that we used to rig up was. If we put any more in we said, "No honey, to the left." She'd be crawling through the concertina and the tangle-foot, all the barbed wire in the world. And this broad would be slinking through it, digging her way through the sand. And she'd get up into the bunker.

And it was funny 'cause she used to charge like ten bucks a hit. But the thing was that if we had screwed her one night and not paid her, she wouldn't have come back.

And this one time we had this broad in there and she was in a tent. And we got hit with rockets. It was fucked up. And we didn't know how to hide her. It was funny as hell.

You couldn't very well leave her there in the tent. 'Cause the lifers check all the tents when you get hit. 'Cause a lot of guys are so fucking lazy they don't give a shit when the incoming starts. They just lie in the rack. They say, "Fuck it. If it hits me, it hits me. I'm going back to sleep." And so lifers make sure everybody's out of the hooch. The way it's set up there's like these little cots and like you couldn't hide her in a tent. It's impossible.

Anyway we hid her. We put a helmet on her and a flak jacket. And she was about five foot three. And we were fucking running out in a group. And the lifer's yelling, "Spread out. Spread out." They were running with her. And we got her out to the bunker, so we piled sand bags over her.

And we were hoping that the alert would go off before daybreak. 'Cause we didn't know how to get rid of her in the daytime. We couldn't very well keep her there all day.

So then this other time this guy C wanted to shoot this whore that used to come in all the time.

He was saying, "If she comes a little closer I'm gonna give it to her."

He's got the machine gun. He's waiting to shoot her. And she wouldn't come in that night. I don't know why. She kept on saying something. She was hollering out to us. And we were saying, "Come on in." And her mother was out there. And her mother was saying something and he says, "Let's fucking give it to her."

He could of got a shot at them at the wire. But like they would've had to explain it. Like if she had come into the wire, what he was gonna do is shoot her. Then take a grenade and throw it out beside her like she was down from the grenade. And she was an enemy sapper.

But the other guys in the bunker didn't want him to kill her because like it would've ruined their good thing. The word would've got out. See her mother was out there. If they had shot her in the wire, and all the people in the vil knew that she used to come and make the visits, then that would've ended the nightly visits and all the little whoopee that we had over there. And it would've sucked.

Up until that time C had never killed anybody. He was fucking pretty upset about it all. He had been in the country three months and never killed anyone. So he wanted to kill her off.

It was the usual stuff. Half the guys that go over there, even in the infantry, are never sure that they killed anyone. And he knew that if he shot her up, the next morning he could go out and look at her. And she'd have been dead. And he would have been sure of it. That wouldn't have been murder to me. That would have been in fun.

I don't know why, but it was funny.

There's a whorehouse in every village. It's so easy. There're whorehouses there 'cause we're there. We've got the money and they've got the bodies. Supposedly. I seen better bodies on ten-year-old kids. I found one whorehouse with a brook underneath it. It was like a Salem commercial. The only thing that sucked was the fucking broads were beasts. A lot of times you go into a fucking whorehouse, they've got all these fucking skin diseases. You just don't want to really touch them. The fucking place looks like a regular orgy scene in the whorehouse 'cause nobody wants to do it face to face.

She's telling you how good you are or telling you that she loves you or somthing. It's so fucking stupid. "I love you" and smells like her fucking feet are coming out of her mouth. Like I want to croak her, you know. "Shut up."

Then you get salty. At first I didn't even fucking kiss them. I'd just fuck them. But then after I was there for a while any type of affection would be nice. Living in your position with nothing but fucking guys and killing people and fucking people trying to kill you. You like a little bit of affection I guess. That must be it. Something to remind you that you're fucking still human.

So then you make out with them and get affectionate and shit. And some of the ones that you make out with would much rather just fuck, to get it over with. 'Cause they don't like you either. And they keep on grabbing you and trying to put it in them. And you're trying to stall it off.

It's so, it's so fucked up. Then you come out and say, what the fuck did I do that for? It's stupid. She made me sick. And I made myself sick and all this other shit.

You go out and get a piece of ass. And it costs you five dollars worth of MPC, which is our money. The Vietnamese aren't allowed to carry MPC. So after you pay for your piece of ass, you just stop them a little bit down the road. And fish them down. And take the MPC away from them.

Mai Li dug me and I thought she was O.K. Because, relatively speaking, she was very attractive. She put the rest of the chicks in the village asleep. But she was just another gook. I sort of had a reserved attitude toward her.

But she was all right. She was fun to talk to. It's nice to talk to a chick once in a while if you're sitting in the fucking mud for a while. You want to go back and talk to the broad. Even if she doesn't understand what you're saying. You know, you sit there and listen to her voice. It makes you feel human. But still the sex thing.

I got pissed off there once. I got off an ammo run. I hadn't been on an operation for a month. And when I came back, I was looking forward to seeing her. It was like going to see a girl. I knew she wouldn't charge me because I hadn't seen her in so long. She'd be happy to see me or she'd put on a front. It didn't matter to me at the time what she was doing.

And I drove by and I told the truck driver to pull up in the center of the vil. And all the whores come running out propositioning everybody in the truck. I looked around and I was yelling for Mai Li. And she come running out and she's waving.

So I jumped off the truck. The big hot reunion. I go inside. She tried to charge me. I got mad.

And she said, "Don't sweat. Take it easy. Take it easy. I'll souvenir you." I said, "O.K." So we went into the hut and I started stripping. And she squatted there in front of me and took a piss.

Now I didn't take into consideration the chick was like

about one step above a savage. No education and no nothing.
She's been living in a grass hut. She doesn't know where she's
at. Or I don't know where I'm at. Or something.

And so I kicked her. I was disgusted.

I said, "You little bitch." And I kicked her.

She was crying. She didn't know what to do. She was
upset. And I felt bad, kind of. She has like a brain of a little
girl, really. She didn't know any better. Like a little girl
wouldn't know any better. She's got to do it. She's got to do
it. I'm sure she hasn't done it since I kicked her. She was
afraid we were all like me, or something. I don't know. I
didn't want to have anything to do with her for a while.

I said, "Screw. Get away from me." She cried and shit.
And went through all the superficial things. And I left.

I went back a week later and she souvenired me for about
two weeks to make up for it. She was all right. I was just
rotten to her. I guess.

## 3. *Marines and Village Children*

There was one time some guy shot at this broad accidentally.

She was about ten years old. He shot her with a .45. He
didn't mean it. It was an accidental discharge. He didn't
think there was a round in the chamber. He was sort of
drunk. So he did it all backwards.

You're supposed to kick out the magazine, and then you
pull a slide back which will eject the cartridge, and then you
look, and you throw it home, and you pull the trigger.

What he did was he threw the slide back, kicked out the
round, let the slide go home, and pulled out the magazine.
Well, he chambered a round without letting the slide go home
because there was a magazine in it. Then he pointed it at the

kid. He was laughing. "I'll kill you, you little fucking gook."

Pulled out the magazine, you know. Let it kind of drop in his lap so she wouldn't see it, 'cause he had his hand there like this. And she was terrified. Fucking blew a hole in her as big as a football. Then he shit.

He said, "What the fuck is going on here?" And he yelled, "Corpsman," and he picked her up and run through the village with her.

And got her in the thing. And the corpsman come down. And the broad died.

I befriended a little kid. He come up to me one day and he gave me a whole box of .45 ammo. He was a ugly little kid. Most of the troops shrug off the ugly kids. And like the ones that are kind of cute they'll give them candy and stuff. He was the ugliest little kid in the world. And he wouldn't ask me for anything. Like most of them sit there and fucking beg you for anything. He never asked me for a fucking thing.

Fixed me up with his sister too. She was a fucking beast. I fucked her, just once, you know, for nothing.

I ate at their house and stuff too. Well, I was supposed to eat. I couldn't eat the stuff. It wasn't bad. It was just that I couldn't trust the food. I'd get sick from it. It smells bad. They use this sauce, lip mau sauce. It's made from dried fishheads and its fucking stench'll kill you. I had a little. They weren't looking, I dumped it. I didn't want to get sick. I didn't really care for them.

The kid was O.K. I remember he gave me the bullets. And then he ignored me. Then one day he was in there with the rest of the kids. It was a garbage run. And he had picked up a can of C-rations: ham and lima beans. This kid was about nine, ten. This kid about fourteen or fifteen grabbed him, took it away from him. So he tried to get it. So the kid started to slap the shit out of him, the older kid.

So then I grabbed the older one by the neck and I said, "Give him back the fucking stuff." So he give it back and he's smiling at me and shit.

But the kid was still scared because he knew he was going to get a beating later. What he was going to do was run home, give it to his parents, knowing he was going to take a beating later. Or else he'd eat it himself: whatever he wanted to do with it. But I knew he was going to take it later.

So I impressed the fact upon his big buddy there that if I hear that he laid a hand on him he'll never be able to come to the dump again 'cause I'll fucking break his legs. Then I kicked him in the ass and I picked him up bodily and threw him off the fucking truck into the garbage heap. And then he fucking just smiled at me again and said, "No sweat, no sweat."

The little kid was O.K. Can't remember his name anymore. I gave him a hat with a corporal insignia on it. And he was a "honcho," which means boss, for a long time. One kid had a staff sergeant insignia. So he was automatically the boss. They see whoever has the most stripes usually tells everybody else what to do. So he had his like own little gang that would do things for him because he had a marine hat with a corporal insignia on it.

And the other kid has staff sergeant. He was sort of leader of all. He was a good kid. They called him L. A. Faggot. Los Angeles faggots are pretty fucking notorious in the armed forces. And he was a cute little kid, so we used to call him L. A. Faggot for the shit of it. And the kid took the name for his own. So you'd ask him what his name was, he'd say, "L. A. Faggot." Another kid was real dark skinned. So we used to call him American Nigger. And you'd ask him what his name was, he'd say, "American Nigger."

And there was another one, Sexy. She was a little girl. And she was so fucking dainty, we used to call her Sexy. She would refuse to fucking fight for food in the dump. She would sit there and sort of look down at all the little kids killing themselves. It was Faggot's sister. And she'd sit there calmly by a tree and Faggot would go get the stuff, fight for it like the rest of the kids, and come back and give it to his sister to sit there and hold. Faggot was a pretty tough kid too, because they didn't fuck with him much.

They used to come over quite often and help us string the barbed wire in a lot of ways. Because they were so small, they could run through the concertina wire without hurting themselves. And their feet were like leather, so they could step on barbed wire. And they used to run a certain strand of wire through it. We used to give them money and C-rations and candy and whatever the hell we could give them.

One day Sexy found an M-79 round that was a dud. And she brought it to the wire and tried to give it to a friend of mine who noticed what it was and tried to get her to pass it over to him real easy. And when she passed it over between the barbed wire it fell and they both ran for it. And then it went off. And she lost some of her fingers.

And so the guys crawled through the wire and grabbed her up and called the medevac and had her evacuated and had her fingers taken with her and everything. And it worked out that she wasn't seriously hurt, like she wasn't crippled or anything. And I guess they sewed her fingers on or something. But she was O.K. She was better off than she would have been.

Maybe not as well off as if she had never found the grenade.

I would give my little friend an apple. 'Cause like the food I'm pretty sure he brought home to his family. Because when I went in their little hut, I seen a lot of C-rations in there. They sort of try to hide it because they know they're not supposed to have the stuff. And they supplement their diet with it. Then he said something to them and so they didn't try to cover it up any more.

They love apples. They love fruit. They don't have apples over there or oranges, things like this. But they're really into apples. And I'd give him an apple 'cause he'll eat that himself.

I wouldn't bring him C-rations. I'd say, "Fight for it like the rest of the kids." He'd sit up in the truck next to me. Eat the apple 'till it was all gone, every bit of it. Then he'd go and fucking fight. Or he'd say hold onto it while he could see what he could get out of the thing. He'd bring the stuff that he got over to me and I'd hold it for him. Cigarettes and things like this.

He smoked. They all smoked. In the C-rations you get like four cigarettes in a little box. Like if it's not my brand I'll throw them away. And there's lots of cigarettes, so they all take up smoking.

And he come back and then he'd hand me all this shit. And he'd get a little pile of junk. And I'd save it for him until he was finished. Then I'd give him his apple and he'd sit there and eat it.

Then he'd take his stuff, put it in a sandbag and leave for home.

A lot of the kids would try to get in the truck and see what they could steal inside the truck. Axes and stuff that you hold underneath the seat, I used to keep a good eye out for that shit. Keep the kids off the truck. He made a lot of enemies.

But he figured my friendship was worth more than a bunch of his friends — his enemies, because they weren't going to give him anything.

## 4. Marines and the Arvn

I remember one time I had been in the country a year by this time. We were going back to regiment in Danang. And the Arvn engineer stopped us at a roadblock.

They bore you to death. They make you sick. They're

trying to be military. So they've got this roadblock up. And they stopped the truck. And the driver is saying, "Get out of our fucking way, you little slopes."

And they come out and they said, "We have a wounded veteran, wounded veteran."

We said, "So what?"

They said, "He doesn't have one leg." He says, "Could you give him a ride up to the hospital?"

So everybody's saying, "Fuck him. Let him hop."

I was in command of the truck. So I said, "Let him on."

I was in the back of the truck. It was a PC three-quarter. So the little bastard comes over on his crutches.

I said, "Throw your crutches up."

So he passed up the crutches. And I grabbed him under the arms and I pick him up and I set him in the seat. The fucking little slope grabbed me by the leg.

And I had been in the country long enough to know that most of them are queer. They hold hands and stuff. And this sort of irks most marines. And we're told that it's a Vietnamese custom, when you're really friendly you should hold hands. So these poor bastards try to hold a lot of guys' hands. So they end up getting beat bloody.

And the guy grabbed my leg. So I got fucking mad. I wasn't in a good mood that morning and I wacked him. And my buddies grabbed his crutches. And I said "Go."

So we took off. We threw his fucking crutches in the rice paddy. And went about another one hundred and fifty yards and threw the other crutch. And then out he went.

That poor fucking bastard was screaming and crying and begging us. "Fuck you, you slope. Out you go."

The Arvn used to wear starched utilities. Everything was just so nice. And like the marines were all slobs. Because we had our clothes washed in rice-paddy water and everything else. Nothing starched.

And they looked like they should be on recruiting posters all the time, you know. We had Arvn security and it started to rain. They went in houses until the rain stopped. So they wouldn't get their uniforms wet.

And left us out there with no security.

One of them had an M-79.

They're not supposed to have them. This was before they rated them. We didn't like it because a lot of them would sell their weapons. This was the rumor, anyhow. That they were selling their weapons to the VC. We weren't fucking happy with the VC having M-79s, a really fantastic fire-power weapon. You can throw a grenade 450 meters, pinpoint accuracy.

And what happened was some grunt was walking along the convoy. They had parked the convoy in the village and they had stopped to take a break. And some marine seen them and started a little hassle.

And one of their officers was walking down. He was a colonel or something, three buttons, major or captain. I forgot their rank insignias. He was walking along the convoy. And the marine was walking down on these mud banks the tanks churn up. Between the mud banks is water and real sticky mud. This stuff is sort of more packed mud, you know solid. So everybody kind of walks on these little mud ridges. And there was a marine on the mud. It was sort of like Robin Hood and Big John, that type of thing. So anyway they all fucking chambered rounds.

The officer in command of troops gave a command, and all the bolts started going home up there. And all the marines that were in the whorehouses grabbed their rifles and went outside. And everybody was like pointing rifles at each other.

Then an American officer come over and said, "You walk in the mud." So the marine walked in the mud.

And he said, "I want your name, your rank and your serial number."

And he apologized to the Vietnamese officer. And they all mounted up and they went out. And everybody was sitting there fucking pissed.

There was eight marines on the patrol and about twenty gooks. So they reached a certain point and they had a rally point. They said, "O.K. we'll go this way, and you go this way."

Before this they had fell into a village the VC were burning. And they went in there and they all chewed them up. And this house was on fire. So they went inside. They were helping put out the fire.

And this mamasan was screaming, trying to get back in there. And the marines were throwing her on her ass and running inside and putting the fire out. So when they come outside, the woman run back in. She kept on straining to go inside.

So they finally said, "Let her go." So she went inside. She come out. And her baby's head was crushed and shit, you know?

The marines were in there putting out the fire but unbeknowing to them they were stomping to death a three-week-old baby.

So this caused uncontrollable laughter among the marines when they found they had accidentally killed a baby. There's nothing else they could do.

And they've got to keep up this pretense of being fucking raving maniacs in order to keep the respect of the monta-

gnards, you know. The gooks think that we're fucking luna-
tics. And you've got to keep this. As long as they're afraid of
us they won't give you a hard time. If they're afraid you'll
shoot them any minute and you don't find anything wrong in
killing.

So the guys start laughing. First it was sort of a nervous
laugh and then they just had a fucking grand time.

Then the one squad had it out after the gooks that had
escaped. The other squad stayed there to put out the fire and
see if there was any of them hiding around and then question-
ing some people.

So they went out after the gooks and it got dark and they set
up. The next morning they had a rally point. This is a place
you come back to if you get hit. And they had two radios. So
they split off and they went in two directions to cover more.

And one unit come under enemy fire. An ambush. So the
only way you can get out of an ambush is to assault it. You
can withdraw. But like you're not out there to get shot at and
then take off. You're out there to kill someone. This is why
we took this long goddamn walk up and down the mountains.
You're not going to let a chance like this slip by. So naturally
the lance corporal who was in charge of this particular squad
said, "O.K., you're on line."

So he yelled to the commander of the Vietnamese to bring
on line assaults. So the four marines get up and they're
pumping away. And all the eight montagnards just sat there
and watched them. Then they ran like hell while the marines
were on line shooting.

So there they are and the radio got shot up. What they had
to do is pull some escape and evasion maneuvers to get away.
The montagnards went back to this rally point where they
had been that morning. The other squad said, "Where's the
marines?" They said, "VC killed them all."

And you segregate: like one marine, three montagnards, one marine, three montagnards.

So the marines were saying, "How come none of you's are dead?"

They said, "We don't know. Too many VC. They just shot marines and we all got lucky."

And all this other shit, you know. So the marines are getting fucking mad as hell. So they're talking and they're saying, "Let's fucking kill them all and we'll screw."

They couldn't figure out a way to do it. They would have to kill all of the gooks. Because one of the other gooks might rat. And they couldn't figure out how they could kill them all. They would have to go out and get the bodies of the other four marines. Now once they got the bodies they could say four of us got it and all the montagnards got it. They were thinking about it and thinking about it.

And one of the gooks was rapping to another one and he started to laugh. And one of the guys turned around and flipped his M-16 on full automatic and was going to start to chop them up. He turned around to shoot them and this other guy hit his rifle.

He says, "No. Not yet."

They grabbed the one that was laughing and punched the fuck out of him and stomped on him for about five minutes. And they threatened the rest of them. "We'll fucking kill you's all."

These Arvn outnumbered the marines. But they were afraid of the marines. And this is what keeps them fighting, is their fucking fear. They're more afraid of the marines than they are of the enemy.

But anyway, the other four marines come back up on the hill and told what happened. So they went back to the base. And when they got back to the base the shit started to hit the fan. They fucking really got into those gooks bad.

I was confused about this because I had thought that montagnards were tough fighters. But the way it strikes me is they're tough enough as long as they're winning. And they hate the VC. They hate the Vietnamese prime and wholly because the Vietnamese consider them savages. Which evokes laughter among all the troops because the troops think that they're all fucking savages.

And I'm sure they think that we're savages.

## 5. Marines and Other Services

I was up in the DMZ and there was a club. The seabees had a club in the base. And the marines were at the club. And some sailors off an LST, these ships that make dock landings and shit, they were there.

This is a fucking very hairy place. 'Cause, the place I was at, Qua Viet, got hit every day and every night too. So everybody's always ducking. And it's a lot of fucking enemy movement, a lot of operations and a lot of fucking guys dying. So it's like really a scary joint.

And these fucking swabbies come off the ship and got drunk down the club. And there was a bunch of grunts down there snuck in. 'Cause the marines aren't allowed to go to other people's clubs. They cannot drink in Army clubs.

We cannot drink in Navy clubs or in Air Force clubs. We have to drink in our own little fucking shitty bunker things that they call "clubs." And you get two beers a day while everybody else can get fucked up. So some marines snuck in there. And the fucking confrontation developed between some marines and some sailors off the ship.

So a fight broke loose. And one of the sailors pulled a blade, and stabbed some marines. And they got gut wounds. They were pissed. When you go to seabee's club you can't be armed. That kind of thing. So they rushed them down to BAS.

And they told some buddies. When we got back to Third Marines there was a battalion force down there: One-Three. First Battalion, Third Marine Regiment. And the guys that knew about it just grabbed their rifles and magazines and put on helmets, fork jackets. They went down there to battle.

I mean it wasn't that they went down there to fucking talk tough just with rifles. They zippered up. They were going to move out. And they ain't no bunch of fucking swabbies armed with pistols, carbines and knives gonna duke it out with a whole bunch of grunts that are armed. I mean they, they went so far as to bring down a machine gun. That whole fucking ship would've been wiped out.

But they were cut off. Battalion CO came down and cooled it before it got started.

This kid, he was driving a truck. This Army lifer come up and chewed him out. D's a good marine. It was in a combined Army-Marine convoy. And it was a rough rider thing. It had to go through enemy-held territory and shit.

So this lifer was giving D the lecture. And D's looking at him, like this isn't my first day in country.

So the fucking lifer went behind the truck. And D released the fucking brake. Rolled the truck back and crushed the fucking lifer between his truck and Jack's truck, and killed him. They couldn't prove he did it on purpose.

Parts of it I remember and parts of it I don't.

Parts of it were told to me in Japan. Like when you're

scared, you're scared. And you just don't remember everything. So it was all fucked up in my mind. Like I didn't know
it was a woman that blew me up until — I don't remember if I
found out in Japan.

What I remember is when I screamed out, "Wire." I remember seeing a glow in the road. And I remember tumble-
saulting. And it was a beautiful feeling. It didn't hurt. I
remember landing.

And then I remember hearing E moaning. So I went over
where he was. I crawled over. And then I realized that my
leg was gone. But I wouldn't look. I didn't look. And I seen
a foot. But I wouldn't look. I didn't want to. I knew it was
gone but I, I didn't want to look. And I got over.

And E was still burning. I was hitting him in the face trying
to put the burns out. That's why I got more burns on this
hand than I did on the other hand. And then I put E on my
back. We crawled out to where there wasn't any fire. And
that's when they all come up.

We had two platoons of Army protecting us during this
mine sweep. And they were all boots in Vietnam. They had
never been fired upon or nothing. So when I screamed "Wire"
and got blown up they're supposed to make a three-sixty
perimeter around us and start firing and then call in for a
helicopter.

Instead they got scared and run down the road away from
us and they come up from the flank behind us. I didn't know
that. I found out later. They come up from the rear. And we
got ambushed from the front. And bullets come from over
behind me. So I started shooting at everybody. I was
panicky.

I found out later that I had hit the Army. Killed four and
wounded three. After I had shot up the Army the white
phosphorous grenade come in.

After we got ambushed, we started going out in the chopper. And the guy on the machine gun got killed. And another bullet come through our helicopter. So I crawled off the stretcher and I grabbed the machine gun and started shooting down at them. They're really a groovy thing. As a matter of fact, I went back down on the corner and everybody was calling me Audie Murphy there for a while. If they had known how scared shit I was. I was just doing things like that to stay alive. I don't remember it. I was shooting at nobody. I was shooting at the dark.

In Japan, when they tried to give me the Silver Star in the beginning I says, "Are you gonna give E back his fucking eyes?" That's what I said. But in reality what I was thinking in my mind was, "Are you gonna give me back my leg?"

And when I was in Chelsea Naval Hospital they were all harassing me because I had spent such a short time in Vietnam. And I had a Silver Star. I was the only one in there that had a, had any, medals.

And the reporters come in and said, "Jesus, it's a very brave thing you did, carrying E out on your back after losing your leg."

I said, "Hey, listen. I got hit with a mine and a phosphorous grenade. And I just didn't want to get fucking hit again. So I threw E on my back for protection."

I don't know if it was true. I think ninety per cent of the reason I pulled him out is the fear of being alone. Fear wants company, you know. You want somebody with you when you're afraid. That's a lousy feeling when you're by yourself.

None of that interview did they print. Well, it was weird I mean like if I had done my job properly, the wire would have been found. And nobody would've got wounded. Nobody.

You're supposed to have two flanks out. On the sides of the roads with these hooks. And they drag these things along.

And if there's a wire there they find them first. And the mine will explode in the middle of the road and nobody will get hurt.

But what the VC were doing was they were setting booby traps on the sides of the roads. And these guys were pulling these poles. And I was losing two guys a day. So I discontinued using the guys. I just didn't want to send any more guys out to die.

Like I felt it was a useless death. And I can't really say that we wouldn't have got wounded because them guys would've probably got hit that day just like they get hit every other day.

But I don't know how I missed the wire. Well, the wire was on the other side of the road. That's how I missed it. But usually I glance at both sides of the road. The wire was on this side of the road. And E spotted it. At that time he is supposed to scream out "Wire." That gives me a chance to get down. And the Army knows what's going on right away. It's just good luck E. One is better than eighty-three or eighty-five, whatever the fuck it was. And he just didn't do it.

He says, "Hey. Come here." I didn't know what the fuck he was saying "Hey. Come here" for. It could have been a fucking broad in the bushes getting laid. It could've been anything. So all the engineers got around. And as I was walking over, I was just about on top of it, I seen it. I said, "Oh, wire." I mean this was the way I was trained. It was the first thing on my mind.

People say to me, "Well, do you think you're a hero?"

"No. I just think that I was conditioned to."

Or, or sometimes I say, "My life isn't worth as much as the eighty guys."

But I don't know if it was conditioning in the Marine Corps, or I don't know if I felt that my life wasn't worth eighty. One thing I do know for a fact: I wasn't a hero.

I mean I didn't do it with any intentions of being a hero. I went to Vietnam with intentions of being a hero. And I didn't do that act to be a hero. Because I didn't want to be a dead hero. And that's just what I thought was going to happen. Boom. I don't know if I did think that was going to. It was too quick. It was just bing: "Wire." Whether it was conditioning because I had went through school and they had pounded in my head all the time to scream out "Wire," I don't know. But E had went through the same schools I went through. But not as long. And he didn't scream out "Wire." So I don't really know.

In Japan I give that reason you're not going to give E's eyes back. At Chelsea I just told them, "I don't want the fucking thing. Get away from me." So they come back. It was kind of a surprise though.

My mother was in one day. And she was all fucking dressed up for something. And my grandmother come in. And my aunt and my uncle. And a colonel come in. And I had just been shot out with dope. And the colonel come over and says, "Well, F is kind of under the weather now so I'll pin his award on you, Mrs. G." And they pinned it on my mother. I knew what they were doing. I just didn't open my mouth. I wanted it. I don't feel that anybody deserves a medal. But I'm glad I did.

The citation said, "While holding mine sweep up Highway 1 on the second day in November, 1967." It was funny because they mentioned "overwhelming enemy forces above and beyond the call of duty." It didn't say screamed out "Wire." What the fuck did it say? Detonated a mine on himself to save the eighty guys. But you know this is what it said in the citation. Something like that. But the idea is there was no overwhelming enemy odds. Because I didn't know they were there yet.

I was fucked up when I was at Chelsea. I told a chaplain

the story what happened.  And I said, "Would you go find out
if it's fact?"  Well, he really went into it.  He was the one that
told me the Army were the ones that hit me with the phosphorous grenade.  It burnt my face.  Some of these burns too.
It's weird when you don't even know your own hero story.
You know parts of it.  You don't know it all.

## 6.  *Marines and Their Officers*

I remember one time when we had a mine sweep and I
found a mine and I blew it and it was a 500 pound bomb —
left a big hole in the middle of the road.  So I called out for
second platoon and I said, "Would you have the second
platoon come out in the dump and fill up the hole on Highway
One so the traffic can pass?"  Second platoon come out there.
There'd been a mine that we missed and the truck got hit with
a mine.  Now second platoon got blowed away; everybody in
the whole truck got wounded.  So we called up the first sergeant to send medevac choppers in to pull them out.  And the
first question he asked was, "How's my truck?"  I mean, how
can you get along with somebody like that?"

☆   ☆   ☆

He's a regular lifer.  He wants everything perfect.  Goes by
the book and nothing but.  One kid actually wrote a letter to
the gunny's wife telling her about his house mouse.  A house
mouse is a gook woman.  She comes and does his laundry and
everything for him.  Just the lifers had them.  This kid really
went out of his way to get him.  He hated him.  Almost everybody hated him anyway.  And he caught him in the rack.  A
hooch has six windows.  We have eight in a hooch and he has
a whole hooch himself.  He had a rug on the floor, air conditioning, refrigerator.  He had everything in there.  Of course,

we have to clean his screens all the time. One night he's peeking in there. Gunny's doing his thing with his house mouse. So he took a picture. And he told gunny's wife everything that he did.

We caught all kinds of hell for that. 'Cause he didn't know who did it. But it was worth it. Oh, was it worth it. He'd make us work a hell of a lot harder and in the sun more. Like we used to work four-hour shifts. And instead of four-hour shifts, he'd have them eight-hour shifts. In that sun you get dizzy. You pass out from sunstroke.

I remember we had an officer. It was about his third day in-country. He wasn't used to the weather. It takes about a few weeks to get used to the climate. It was real hot out then. And we went out on a patrol.

And he got heat stroke. They had to medevac him. It was really funny. Because we did it. We moved out a little bit faster than we should have.

Our CO rotated. He was an alcoholic. He didn't care. The executive officer could care less about anything. He was always fucking around you know on all these stupid little errands and getting the administration and it all put together. And the CO was sitting in the tent drunk. He was cool. So anyway, our CO rotated and our XO rotated and we got two assholes from Eight-inch Battery. They call them "pretty battery."

Anyway, it was in the monsoons and it was like causing little rivers or rivulets right from the position. So we kind of just walked through them or jump over them at certain points

when it wasn't that wide. You know you're soaking wet
anyway. Well, he made us build a little wooden bridge over
various parts of the battery. Red and white. Red and white
bridges. Right out of some god damn geisha house, you know.

What he did was bet the CO of Eight-inch a case of beer
that within thirty days our outfit, his outfit that he takes
command of, would look better. There's also a Bronze Star
given out for the most beautiful position. And we weren't too
happy, with this being a combat unit. We were pretty pissed
off. He decided that our position was fucked up. The gunny
didn't care about pretty things. He just wanted us to be a
fucking effective fighting unit.

That's when the shit started to hit the fan. We started
having war calls which is like at midnight everybody in the
outfit starts opening fire screaming, "Gooks in the wire." In
the barbed wire fences. And then you try to kill any of the
lifers that you didn't like.

So we tried to get the CO a couple of times with a machine
gun. One time his rack took nine holes. His cot; nine bullet
holes. He dove out of it and got away. Everybody would be
shooting so he couldn't check weapons.

And they'd be throwing grenades at the wire and shit and
yelling, "Gooks in the wire. Gooks." And they'd blow the
siren and then run around. And then half the guys would be
facing out where it's shooting. The other half of the guys
would be waiting for a lifer to come out of the tent.

The only one that didn't give a fuck about us war-calling
was the gunny. He was crazy. And he's walking along the
brim with his grease gun. We kind of liked him. We didn't
like him but we kind of respected him, you know?

One time the guys on the fifty tried to get the CO when he
was coming up behind them. Turns around and shot the fifty
and got two rounds out before the fucking thing jammed.

And the gunny thought it was a grease gun. He said, "Who is on that machine gun?"

"Gunny, we thought you were gooks."

He said, "Get down here, you little fucking turd."

He was a little maggot himself. Little Italian guy. He's a tough prick. And CO knew his number was up.

War call is used to tell the lifers that you don't like being fucked with. You shoot up and have a grand time. But the more they fucking shot up his hooch, the fucking rougher he got.

The gunnery sergeant and the first sergeant had requested mast to the Third Marine Amphibious Force. Request mast is going up the chain of command to make a complaint. They were requesting mast on behalf of the troops in the battery saying that they're suffering undue troop harassment. And when a lifer does it they know there's something wrong.

That fucking fool made us build him a porch outside of his tent. And he had an umbrella sent from the States. He would sit there and sip drinks and stuff and overlook his domain. While the fucking guys would be out there killing themselves.

Not only did we have to fire support on operations and fire harassment-fire all night long while we're in position, but we had to work. Like one time he wanted the whole berm moved up fifty yards. He wanted to enlarge the position. This would entail picking up all the wire barricades that we put up: concertina wire, tangle-foot, aprons, all this. This takes a lot of time, you know, and a lot of cut hands and shit. And that all had to be pulled up and moved out. We were fucking ripping. We knew it was stupid. He brought the empo tractors out and shone the spotlights on us while we were working at night. And this is also endangering our lives.

So one night this guy named H booby trapped his tent. And in the morning when he woke up it wasn't the CO that got it.

It was the executive officer, Captain J. Captain K was the one we wanted to get. He was a fucking asshole. But J, it was just as good to get J 'cause he sucked too. They both sucked.

The way the trip went was this. When they opened the tent they would pull the pin on the grenade. There was two TNT supplementary charges tied to the grenade which is two pounds of TNT. That would entail four pounds of TNT and about a half a pound of composition B inside the grenade and shrapnel and stuff. Well anyway, it blew off both his legs, it blew up his crotch, it blew up the side of his face, three fingers on one hand, and puckered him with shrapnel and stuff.

They threatened to press charges against the whole outfit for mutiny. They were trying to figure out a way they could fucking keep it hush-hush. Nobody wants to know the Marine Corps mutinied. They were flooding the unit with the Criminal Investigating Department. You can tell because they were supposed to be all shit birds — the fuck-ups who never do it right. You can tell they're CID because they talk about doing all this stuff. Yet they don't smoke dope. They weren't fooling too many people. And they were censoring all our mail. CID was responsible for that. Which is a no-no. But they did it.

They finally did convict H. The CO was transferred to some pussy thing up in Division. They took him away from a command unit.


## 7. *Marines and Each Other*

I got transferred later on in the War to this place called OP [Observation Post] Hawk. And there was a place called OP Panther. And the next one to that was way up. It was OP Eagle, right? These three looked into the three valleys near the enemy infiltration routes. And they put MPs up there with these BC scopes, which is like super powerful binoculars on tripods to watch this frigging village. And they had a radio. There's a war on, right?

And this one post was used for twofold purpose of watching enemy infiltration routes with the regular troops. And watching troop movements down in that village to see if any of those guys went to the hooch. And then they'd immediately radio an MP jeep in hiding like a mile down the road and say, "They're in there." And their fucking things would come fucking flying. And the poor guys were in there getting laid. Jumped out. They run in.

"O.K. C'mon. Hurry it up." Or "Get out," you know. And that kind of shit.

And the guy's saying, "Oh, have a fucking heart."

And they'd arrest him. And take him back down. And you'd have to stand office hours for it and you could lose a rank. It was unbelievable.

They fucking put an MP unit up there to watch them twenty-four hours a day. We didn't know about it. Like everyone was getting busted down there. We were saying, "How the fuck do them MPs know we're down there?"

But the way we found out, this guy got friends with this kid. We called him Chief. He was an Indian kid from I forget where. And he got sent to my gun. And he was in the MPs.

He told our provost marshal, "If you fucking think that I'm going to sit there and tell line troops that they're on the wrong side of the street, that their shoes aren't shiny and that they're wearing either unserviceable or . . ." what the hell do they call it? There's a word they use in the service for like wearing stuff that's not issued to you. It's one of their silly little laws. Like you can't wear certain things because it takes away from your uniform and shit. For Christ's sake nobody had any knees in the trousers; their ass was hanging out. They're worried about if their shoes are shined. And he was saying, "I refuse to do it."

The MPs make out pretty good over there. They're bastards. Like they raid whorehouses. And those poor broads
like work all day. They make a lot of money though. They
average like three hundred a week, American currency.

And the MPs raid the place. They take all their money
away. The poor bitches split the money up among the kids and
kids all scatter in different directions. It's funny to watch a
raid. And the Vietnamese police pull up with them. So the
money's confiscated. So the MPs turn in two hundred and put
a hundred in their pocket. Send it home by money order.

Like this one guy, a corporal, was telling me his wife
bought a car. He says, "Hey. I've got to stay over here. I'm
making too much money here." He says, "I can't afford to go
home." His wife had bought a lot of stuff for their apartment.
And they were like saving up for a house and stuff. That
money was going to go to a Vietnamese orphanage or a club
fund somewhere. And the fuck. They figured they'd skim the
top.

'Cause they had a quota. The MPs had a quota. The poor
bastard had that village had to bust everybody that went in
there or have a good reason why not. 'Cause those guys up in
the top of the hill. One of them was a lifer. And they knew
he'd log out. Every time you make a call you log it in. You
say, "Have called Mobile Patrol. And have sicked them on
troops fraternizing." He gets good rank if they bust a hundred
marines. They all get fined. The money goes to Vietnamese
orphanages and club funds and stuff like that. See they'll take
like a hundred dollar fine off you and maybe take a stripe
away.

We had one guy shooting at MPs. That shook their shit.
This black kid. They shot at him first. He was in a village
and, well, it was in Indian country. And he was in there. He
was getting laid. He was coming out. And they were going in.

They said, "Halt."

He said, "Fuck you." He started running. So they chased him. So he went through the village. And then he run over into the tree line. And he's running his ass off. And he run right across the rice paddies. And they come out. They said, "Halt." And they fired a warning shot in the air. He kept on running. He said, "They're not going to shoot me for getting laid."

They shot another round in the rice paddies right next to him. So he could see the water spread up and hear the round cross by him.

He had a grease gun. He turned around and shot right back at them. That fucking ceased that shit, boy. They all were ducking and grabbing cover. And he just kept on running.

There was a big thing about that too. They come running up there. They had a captain come up, MP captain. "You were shooting at my men."

They were overstepping their authority anyway. They were supposed to be taking prisoners back. And they decided to be assholes and pin somebody else to make some points. He wasn't kidding either. He's great. I forget his name. He was a mailman. He was like twenty-six or something. He was a mailman from Virginia. Black guy. Worked for the Post Office. And he was in the Marine Reserves. Decided to go active for the war. For the shit of it.

Like one time L chased a prostitute across a rice paddy in a five-ton truck. And stuck the truck in the rice paddy. Jumped out and was going to shoot the bitch. I can't remember the reason for that. I remember he wanted to marry a gook prostitute in the vil. He was serious. That was the unfortunate part about it.

We all went, "Look man, she's a prostitute."

He says, "No. She's a widow. Her husband was killed. He was in the Vietnamese Marines." And all this other shit.

He used to buy her stuff, fucking cigarettes and perfume. Things like this. It was tough to get perfume too. You'd give them Right Guard and stuff. They use it as perfume. After-shave they use as perfume. They have to bathe in rice paddies. The water really smells. It's swamp water.

We says, "She's fucked more people than you have."

He said, "She has not. She probably lied and had a couple of other people."

We said, "Yeah, she probably had a couple of other people in the morning before you meet her, and a couple of more people after you leave. Cut the shit."

And so to prove a point, half the outfit went down and fucked her.

And it sort of upset him. So he asked permission to marry her anyway. And of course they fucking denied it. They were going to send him to the DMZ. And that didn't work. So they ended up sending him to the brig for some other charge.

I was working as a radio operator. We had this officer plot the map wrong. We were a landing zone. And you send your patrols out looking, like search-and-destroy missions. He moved them from checkpoint three, and he plotted the map wrong. And then an observer got on our freq and asked us where our men were. The lieutenant called in and told them where he had the map plotted. So he called back to Danang and got an air strike.

They dropped napalm that killed the whole platoon. Eigh-teen guys. I felt like I was responsible. I felt bad because they were my friends.

A quota come in for in-country R and R. I was supposed to stay two days and I stayed twenty-seven. I went AWOL. I had to. My head was really out of place. But they didn't think so. They gave me battalion office hours. Busted me.

I should've never went AWOL, they said. They said, I "should've took it like a marine." The same exact words. I can remember, "Should've took it like a marine."

# CHAPTER II

# Court Martials about the War

INSOFAR AS THESE are not traditional war stories, they are more likely to be true. And insofar as they are not traditional stories, it matters less if they are not true. Because if the preceding narratives were invented, they would still be useful for what they say about the men that invented them. The main reason for including the narratives has not been to show the War as it was, but rather as it was seen. However, what might be considered one of the most implausible of these narratives was confirmed in every detail by a court martial transcript. Lance Corporal David Hurley was found guilty of setting a booby trap that blew up his executive officer.

Hurley had been an ideal candidate for the Marine Corps. While attending high school in Lynwood, California he won eleven letters in sports and served on the student government. During his two years of college he worked for the National Biscuit Company. His supervisor there sent a recommendation on the eve of the court martial:

> While I was unintentionally out of sight, a fellow deliveryman approached Dave, who was loading trucks with cookies. A conversation started and the deliveryman, a good friend of Dave's, asked Dave to throw a couple of extra cases of chocolate chip cookies on the load — "Nobody would know the difference" was the deliveryman's plea. Dave politely refused.

Another reference was provided by the family minister:

I have observed the positive qualities of integrity, honesty, kindness, stability and spirituality develope (sic) and grow through these years. At no time has he ever exhibited the rebelliousness and wild spirit all too frequently to be seen in some of our youth.

He became an ideal marine. A sergeant testified that Hurley:

was always a hard worker, sir, first to get up and get out and do it. He would go out and help people in the guns. We're short there, and he did this just all on his own, sir. I think he is an outstanding marine, sir. He never seemed to give anybody any trouble about anything. He'd get up and do his job. You could give him responsibility to get a job done, sir, and you can be sure that it would get done, sir. It wasn't like a lot of people, you give them a job and that's about as far as it goes, then you have to have somebody else do it.

His lieutenant also testified during the court martial:

Lance Corporal Hurley carried out his duties in an excellent manner. He worked many extra hours and always maintained a cheerful, eagerness (sic) and willing attitude towards his work. I would be glad to have Lance Corporal Hurley work in my section at any time.

The commanding officer had been transferred from another gun battery where, according to testimony, "They had his hut booby trapped already, that it was rigged to be set off with a wire, and it would be done by someone on watch." The commanding officer was transferred in time; but again, as one of his men at the new assignment testified, "The general feeling in the battery was that they were pushing stuff on the battery that wasn't necessary." According to the testimony of another enlisted man, the decision to set a booby trap was the result of "a general feeling."

"Fraggings" were a form of guerrilla warfare conducted by the enlisted men against their officers. In this case the grenade was rigged so that it would appear to be the work of the Viet Cong. The blame would be harmlessly shifted if the deception succeeded. At the same time, marines became the Viet Cong. Or at least they became marines trying to become the Viet Cong.

Hurley used a technique of the Viet Cong, but without their usual success. He missed the intended target. By most accounts, it was the commanding officer that he was trying to blow up. Instead, his victim turned out to be the executive officer. The fact that Hurley was eventually arrested represented another failure. Although a prolonged investigation was necessary, he was not mistaken for a Viet Cong.

The grievances against the commanding officer suggested that he had even more difficulty than his men in adapting to guerrilla warfare. A conspicuous and fixed gun battery, such as he commanded, was itself incompatible with the necessities of this combat. His men felt he compounded the inherent hazards of their position. One of the ways he created an aesthetically pleasing base was to have the enlisted men line up their tents with aiming stakes. This precision in turn made it easier for the Viet Cong to aim their mortar attacks.

Just as David Hurley was not an aberrant marine, the enlisted men in his unit were not aberrant in their endorsement of the fragging. Another court martial transcript contains a reference, provided by the Criminal Investigating Department, to "over twenty" fraggings that occurred during the first eight months of 1969 within the Third Division. There were at least as many in the other marine division in Vietnam, the First, according to a "confidential message" from the Commanding General of the Third Marine Amphibious Force. The Third Division contained four per cent of the total American force in Vietnam at that time. By projecting, the over twenty cases becomes over five hundred cases during the first eight months of 1969. Although the over twenty fraggings were evenly spread across the eight months, by September, 1969, there were only two arrests. A large reason for this failure of the Criminal Investigating Department is that fraggings had the wide support of enlisted men who were unwilling to assist the investigations. When the fraggings were solved, it was usually with the greatest difficulty — as in the Hurley case.

There was a widespread tendency for enlisted men to hold the view that their vulnerability to the VC and NVA was maximized by American officers. Unnecessary risks were readily defined in a war where, as one defendant in a fragging case explained, "Sometimes we knew what we were fighting for; sometimes we didn't." However much the officers may have contributed to the danger, the source of the danger was the VC and NVA. But the VC and NVA were viewed as simply doing their job. They therefore were not blamed for the losses that they inflicted on the marines. Instead, the blame shifted to the officers (as well as Arvn and villagers) who, it was thought, were making it easier for the VC and NVA to do their job by not providing sufficient protection from them. In other words, the officers were viewed as not doing their job.

Private Clyde Smith, Jr. testified at a court martial about his grievances against a marine lieutenant:

We went on a mine sweep one day and I come out of the rice paddies ahead of the mine sweepers, you know, which I was supposed to do because I was walking the flank. I came out about two hundred yards ahead of the rest of them and they were taking their time and they were really slow about it and I was standing at the edge of the field waiting for them to come and he come rushing up to me and starts calling me all kinds of foul language and stuff like this and tells me that he hopes I step on a

booby trap, you know, and get killed or something. So we ex-
changed words and stuff like this, you know. I kept telling him
to stay off my back.

Later, in an interview, Private Smith explained that his pace
was the result of discovering that "a lot of guys get killed
lagging around." He believes it was an argument he had with
the lieutenant that led to his being assigned to walking the
flank. His assumption is based on new arrivals normally getting this assignment, whereas he had been in Vietnam for
seven months at that point. A fragmentation grenade exploded outside the officers' lounge of B Company, Seventh
Engineer Battalion on May 30, 1970. The lieutenant was in
the lounge at the time, but a different officer was wounded.
Private Smith pleaded guilty.

In another court martial, Private Reginald Smith testified
that his marine lieutenant delayed setting up a listening post
during Operation Dewey Canyon. By the time three men
were finally sent out for this purpose, the North Vietnamese
Army had "set up their .30 caliber automatic and everything.
They were just sitting there waiting." Two of the three men
were killed. This was among the grievances discussed by the
troops shortly before the lieutenant was killed with a fragmentation grenade.

In most cases, the victims of fraggings were officers whom it
was thought had been in the Marine Corps either not long
enough or else too long. Clyde Smith, Jr. complained that his
newly arrived lieutenant "went by the book." This literal
mindedness was offered as an explanation for the inability of
the lieutenant to adapt to the unexpected requirements of
guerrilla warfare. The career noncommissioned and commis-
sioned officers were also seen as inflexible in a context that
required flexibility. For it was thought their military ways had
been set through participating in, or absorbing the folklore of,
more conventional wars. The lieutenant of Reginald Smith

was a "mustang"; that is, he had been promoted after extended service as a noncommissioned officer.

The elaborate technology with which the military surrounded its troops in Vietnam meant that the Americans were encumbered in a guerrilla war where it was necessary to be unencumbered. For the troops using technology, mobility was limited instead of enhanced. For the troops supplying technology, there were related problems due to the nature of both it and guerrilla warfare. The facilities that were necessary to maintain the technology involved a proliferation of men, together with matériel, that were in the midst of combat but unable to engage in it. Eight to one is the ratio that is officially given of support troops to combat troops. The movement of support troops was confined by the defenses around their facilities. The confinement made both them and the matériel easy targets for the VC and NVA. Although they were exposed to the dangers of combat, they could do even less than the combat troops about these dangers.

In turn, the marines providing support sought easy targets for manageable issues. The target and issue were easily identified at the Maintenance Battalion of the Force Logistic Command, north of Danang. For technology was enmeshed with another aspect of American society that had been re-created in Vietnam. Racial conflict was a dominant theme of life within the battalion. Black marines held a succession of meetings where they discussed their principal grievances: restrictions on the length of afros, the absence of soul music on the jukebox at the enlisted man's club, and what were considered lighter sentences in disciplining whites.

The officers were accused of discrimination, but it was the white enlisted men who were considered the beneficiaries. Several black enlisted men who attended a meeting on February 5, 1970, recalled discussing various means "to get rid of the beasts." Later that evening, blacks summoned blacks from the enlisted man's club. A grenade exploded shortly afterwards that killed one white and wounded sixty-two others.

A black sergeant was referring to discrimination when he wrote his argument for a change of venue in the court martial of the enlisted men charged with fragging the club: "I have had problems and did go for help, but got no help. I have talked with people of higher rank and not one thing has been done."

One of the defendants had, according to a fellow enlisted man, prepared a list of complaints and

> wanted to see General Padalino about the problems. I don't know if he actually got to see the General, but I know he went to see someone. When he came back he was all pissed off and started talking about "The command doesn't want to help us." He said, "We tried to play The Man's game his way. Now we are going to do it our way."

The day after the club had been grenaded, General Padalino sent a memorandum "to all hands" that asked:

> What cause was served? What possessed the perpetuator (sic) of this henious (sic) act? What possible motive could lead a man to commit this wanton deed? Answers of course stagger the imagination.

An additional response by the command acknowledged the state of war within the battalion. As the personnel officer testified:

> The day following the grenading, all the officers were called together at the staff club. We were told to come armed. We were informed by Colonel Morin what had happened. Apparently he thought it was so serious, though, that we had to conduct an immediate shake-down. We had to conduct the shake-down armed.

Four days later, Colonel Morin issued a memorandum to the troops that explained the reasoning behind this search for what he referred to as "unauthorized weapons or ordnance (sic)":

I know that most of you are concerned about the small percentage of people who are on pot, dope, harbor tools of death, fraternize with VD-infected prostitutes and generally refuse to do anything that is productive — you can bet that I am likewise concerned but you can help me to stop this spread of hate and discontent by standing up for what is right. Which side are you on?

Alert is still the word for TET season — we all will live longer.

Three days later, another colonel issued another memorandum. He announced another attempt at disarming the troops. "Amnesty boxes" would be provided so that "unauthorized weapons" could be turned in "without fear of prosecution or reprisal." His other innovation coincided with a concern about crime in the streets that was then prevalent in the United States:

Further searches and lighting of the area will take place when needed to guarantee the safety of the Marines of this Battalion. I will not allow a condition to exist wherein a man cannot walk down the company street at night without fear.

Meantime, a fragmentation grenade exploded in the hooch of four noncommissioned officers located in the same area as the enlisted men's club. A black private, Ronald McDonald, was found guilty of the fragging on April 7, 1970. The incident occurred on February 11, the day after Colonel Morin had suggested that "those of you who want kicks can get out there and take your kicks at Charlie." Although Colonel Morin was presumably referring to the Viet Cong,

Charlie was one of the terms by which black marines referred to white marines.

Private McDonald was sentenced to eighty years. The sentence was seen by blacks at the base as further evidence of discrimination. Of the four noncommissioned officers in the hooch, two were uninjured, and two received superficial wounds. Whereas Hurley, who was white, had been sentenced to seven years for gravely wounding his executive officer.

CHAPTER III

# Inverted Warfare

WHILE VIEWING VIETNAM from the United States, there has
been a tendency for civilians to see the actions of American
combatants toward the Vietnamese as the result of racism and
impersonalization. But racism would not explain why there
was a high regard for the Viet Cong and North Vietnamese
Army (VC/NVA) who are racially indistinguishable from
the Army of the Republic of South Vietnam (Arvn) for
whom there was a low regard. Nor would impersonalization
explain why there was substantial hostility directed against the
Arvn with whom there was personal contact, and little or no
hostility toward the more remote VC/NVA. A reconciliation
of these apparent inconsistencies should suggest the depth of
disorientation imposed by this guerrilla war.

In the case of marines, the beginning of an explanation
could be found in boot camp. Homosexuality appeared in two
contradictory themes of basic training. On the one hand,
homosexuals were the enemy. Referring to navy corpsmen in
general, and one in particular, a former marine explained:

A lot of them were like prissy. I mean looked on the faggoty-
type side. You could tell they were corpsmen. But I mean if that
guy was in marine boot camp he'd of got bounced out. Or he'd
have so many problems within the system that he fucking

wouldn't be able to hack it. He'd go out of his mind. He'd be called "a faggot."

On the other hand, marine recruits were called "faggots" by their drill instructors during boot camp. By compelling these men to accept such labels, the drill instructors achieved on a psychological level the same control that they had on a physical level when, for example, the men were not all allowed to defecate during the first week of boot camp.

As defined by the boot camp experience, homosexuality was just incidentally a sexual condition. More important, it represented a lack of all the aggressive characteristics that were thought to comprise masculinity. This connection between passivity and homosexuality was vivid to the marines in boot camp since they were unable to combat the label and the activities surrounding it. When a recruit mentioned that he and a friend had been separated in violation of the "buddy system" under which they joined, the drill instructor is reported to have asked, "Do you like Private X?" The next question was "Do you want to fuck him?"

After sending six men into a small shower room, the drill instructor, in another account, shouted

"Everybody on your back." We're all nude. So you fall on top of each other. You get assholes in your face. And then they turn on cold water and they make you run out and stand there.

This ritual, like most others in boot camp, was coupled with violence. As the men left the showers, the drill instructors "beat your fucking head in."

The violence towards trainees was merged with their learning how to do violence, so that "we used to be disgusted with the other services because we considered them unaggressive." Aggression meant learning how to protect not only their lives, but also their masculinity. Accordingly, after boot camp they referred to the Marine Corps as "the crotch," while the other military branches were called "the sister services."

The overreaching lesson of boot camp had been that combat must be on the marines' terms. This point was made by the drill instructors in a way that led one veteran to recall: "You just get shit on all the time if you don't live by their rules. If you don't, they'll screw you any way they can." One of these accepted rules involved the rationale for this training, "They have to do it to protect your lives if you're going in combat." Boot camp training was continually linked to Vietnam by such means as reminding the recruits of the date they would be arriving there and by indicating the number of casualties that would result "if you don't take the training seriously." Throughout, it was made clear that training on the drill instructors' terms would in turn make the VC/NVA fight on the marines' terms.

Yet, in Vietnam, the marines discovered that the VC/NVA "fight on their fucking terms, not on ours," according to another veteran. Considerable effort was directed at getting the VC/NVA to fight on the marines' terms. "What we tried to do is fucking chase them around so they don't know what's going on. But it's never that way." The VC/NVA not only refused to fight on the marines' terms, but by fighting according to their own terms they made the marines' terms inoperable. The link that was established between boot camp and Vietnam reappeared to hinder rather than help morale. For instead of the promised discontinuity between the two settings, the marines vis-à-vis the VC/NVA bore an unexpected similarity to the recruits who were called "girls" by the drill instructors.

The ascendance of the VC/NVA's terms was possible in large part because these terms were unknown to the marines. Even after locating the VC/NVA, their intentions were unclear:

It depends on where they want to fight. You never know if they want to fight there and get that one company and consider it a day. Or if they want to just really get out of there. You can't tell. Or if they're just sucking you into one big mob scene.

The last of these possibilities, that there were other VC/NVA waiting in ambush, was the governing one. It meant that the marines were never able to assume any correspondence between the VC/NVA they saw and the ones that saw them.

Because the marines were seen in their totality, their intentions were open. Their terms were correspondingly weakened. For the VC/NVA were given an opportunity to develop counter-terms: "They know every map square where they can hold a good defense. Where there's a lot of heavy brush that would be tough for us to move our heavy equipment in."

Some of the problems that arose from trying to prepare men who were still in the United States for Vietnam were inherent to using a low risk artificial setting to anticipate the high risk real one. Training in the United States did not pass for combat in Vietnam: "When they used to send us out we used to go make believe we set up an ambush and make believe someone walked by. You knew when all this shit was over you got to get to bed. So I mean it's not good." Just as combat in Vietnam does not pass for training in the United States: "You're not sitting there in 'Nam saying to yourself: 'Let me think now, the instructor told me to do it this way.' What the hell!"

The deeper problems that arose had less to do with training for wars in general than with this war in particular. Booby traps caused a majority of deaths in Vietnam. But booby trap training was regarded as a contradiction in terms:

> They show you all the booby traps and stuff. What's good showing you the booby trap? I mean, if you find a booby trap, the odds are good you ain't going to see it 'til after it blows up.

Efforts to simulate a Vietnam in the United States suffered from a more general handicap: "How can you train a person to fight someone that they've been fighting for so long and they haven't done good enough a job to find out anything about them?" Training in the United States, then, was futile for the same principal reason that combat in Vietnam was to be futile for the marines. So the difficulty of anticipating the VC/NVA through training in the United States was at least one authentic reconstruction of the setting to be found in Vietnam. Also, the apparent unreality of training in the United States may not have been entirely inappropriate preparation for Vietnam. The above example of marines setting ambushes for other marines was said to be "make belief," but it anticipated the internecine character of the War.

The military techniques of the VC/NVA compelled the marines to violate their own traditions. These traditions were not abstractions. They were reasons for being. They also provided a set of expectations for Vietnam. But after arriving there, it turned out they had no application when "you can't go in and kick the ass where you could in other wars." Here is the process of discovery:

> When I first got there, two VC held down the whole platoon just by firing over our heads. Then word was passed out, "Stay down. Don't waste rounds. They'll just do this for fifteen minutes and leave." And being a new guy and thinking how the marines are supposed to be so tough, I said, "Why don't we go get them?" But, of course, they knew what they were doing. We probably would've went and got them. There probably would've been booby traps all over the place. And we would've probably lost another twenty guys getting two. So we just sit there and stay for fifteen minutes, twenty minutes, until they got tired.

When they arrived in Vietnam, these men had belonged to the Marine Corps for about eight months. This is a short time to become deeply involved in traditions — even allowing for

the intensity of the boot camp experience. The commitment
to the traditions of the Marine Corps was largely a result of
their coinciding with the traditions of the street corners to
which these men had belonged before their enlistment. The
interchangeability of the traditions could be seen when the
same marine who was "thinking how the marines are supposed
to be so tough" later described his experience with the
VC/NVA through a street corner analogy: "That's like some
guy walking up to you and punching you in the face every
night and then before you have time to turn around or put up
your hands he's gone."

The previously clear and central distinction between aggressiveness and passivity was lost for the marines when they
arrived in Vietnam. They found thmselves using aggressive
means which had passive results. Meantime, the VC/NVA
used passive means which had aggressive results.

The passive aspects of the VC/NVA took a variety of
forms. To begin with, the VC/NVA did not fit any of the
traditional American notions of what a formidable adversary
should look like. They were the wrong size. Sometimes they
were the wrong sex. They wore the wrong clothes, since the
VC and occasionally the NVA lacked uniforms. They even
wore the wrong expression: "It's hard to look through an
Oriental person. They could probably hate your guts and stab
you in the back, but they'll always smile at you." The more
passive they appeared, the more difficult it was to defend
against their aggression.

The marines heard lectures about the Vietnamese man
expressing friendship with other men through physical contact. But this behavior became all the more inexplicable as a
result of the lectures. For if hand-holding between men was a
custom, it meant — as far as the marines were concerned —
that these gestures were not deviations within the Vietnamese

society; rather the whole society was deviant. A marine recalled that

> we had classes before we went over. That's just their way of
> life. Like them holding their arm on another guy means they're
> friends. It don't mean — that's what we were told anyways.

Nevertheless, in Vietnam "most of us" believed it did mean
they were homosexuals.

The marines needed an explanation that would enable them
to relate these male gestures to their own culture, not that of
the Vietnamese. This was possible by defining it as homosexuality, since it was a familiar category to marines. By
placing the Arvn in it, his behavior ceased to be strange.
Equally important, the marines understood what their own
behavior ought to be in response:

> The Arvn walk down the street holding each other's hands. Or
> they'll come up to you and they'll put their hand on your leg.
> And you sucker them. Because as far as we're concerned, they're
> queer.

In more important ways, the classification of Arvn as
homosexuals was not based on their presumed sexual activity. The fact that Arvn were living at bases with their wives
contributed to the belief they were homosexuals. For the presence of wives meant the Arvn led a soft life. Hence they were
not, to use a common marine term, "hard."

In the same way, the fact that Arvn did not attempt to
engage in homosexual activity with the marines was an additional ground for believing the Arvns were homosexual. For
it was thought that fear, a sign of homosexuality, deterred
them: "They wouldn't fool around with us anyway. They
wouldn't even look at us the wrong way, 'Cause they knew
how good we were, which I thought we were."

A literal interpretation of the war by the marines, among

other results, would have made them allies of the Arvns. But
the Arvn provided the model for a less literal approach that
released the marines from whatever obligations remained to
define them as allies. It was thought the Arvn interpreted the
War out of existence: "They don't want nothing to do with the
War, but yet it's their war."

The reluctance of Arvn to engage in combat was treated as
interchangeable with fighting on the side of the VC/NVA. A
marine who regarded the Arvn as homosexuals, "every one of
them," cited as evidence: "They're just too scared where there
is gooks. Where the gooks are, they go in the opposite direction. They don't want to go out and make contact with them
at all." A related assumption was expressed by another
marine who considered it just as likely they would go in the
same direction as the VC/NVA: "I heard if you get a patrol
of Arvn with you, and if they're getting beat, they'll just go
right on the opposite side. And they'll shoot at you instead of
with you. Kind of get scared."

An official ethonology was the response of the Marine
Corps to a feeling among the marines that "we didn't like the
idea of us fighting for an army of faggots." Specifically,

> You hear the propaganda report, you know, our bullshit. Like
> public relations between us and the Vietnamese. Well our public
> relations give us propaganda material telling us how the Viet-
> namese are a proud, simple people and courageous. And give
> us history of the country and how they fought the Chinese and
> everybody. And the Vietnamese war heroes and all this other
> shit. To impress upon us the fact that they're really not fucking
> gutless bastards. But we all knew better and we used to just hate
> them all the more. The more they tried to justify the Vietnamese,
> the more we didn't like them.

The troops were not in a situation that they thought lent
itself to this or any other form of intellectualizing. What did
matter was that where the marines were vulnerable to attack

from the VC/NVA they became the passive party, and the
Arvn were seen contributing to this vulnerability. In at least
one sense, the marines were more passive vis-à-vis the
VC/NVA than the Arvn were. The marines had their passivity imposed upon them by the VC/NVA, while it was often
thought the Arvn acted passively through their own volition.

At times, the marines worked almost as actively at making
themselves the enemy of the Arvn as they did at making the
Arvn their enemy. The first process recreated the theme of
boot camp that violence should be done for one group so that
they might do violence to a second group. There was a con-
sensus among marines that Arvn had nothing to fight for:
"They didn't give a shit." The marines tried to give them
something to fight against by making themselves the foremost
enemy of the Arvn. As the marines found it increasingly
difficult to establish a direct link between means and intended
ends, they resorted to these indirect links.

In short, one reason the Arvn became the enemy was that
the marines were, after all, bound to them as allies. For the
ineffectiveness of the Arvn in combat meant the task of the
marines was that much greater and more dangerous: "Most of
the time when they did get into contact they always got their
ass kicked. And we usually had to come in and help them
out."

But the marines were bound to the Arvn in a more immedi-
ate way. They provided the marines with a means of trying to
salvage a disrupted frame of reference. For the Arvn were
proof that there was, after all, a connection between passivity
and homosexuality. The marines were not only able to focus
on them as passive targets, they could act against them aggressively.

Locating homosexual Arvn was a welcome relief from
having to cope with an often unrecognizable and always
evasive VC/NVA. There were no problems identifying the

homosexuality of the readily available Arvn. The identifica-
tion was based on criteria that did not require scrutiny or
interrogation. The proof was an impression:

> We thought a lot of them were queer, because of the way they
> act. They were so, I don't know, prissy like and awkward. And
> just the way they laughed and looked at you.

However, the assaults against assumed homesexuals were in
no sense a charade. They were more a form of warfare than
an alternative to it. All that kept the beatings from escalating
was a lack of resistance by the Arvn:

> The Arvn lieutenant told his men, "The next time a marine hits
> you, I want you to shoot him." So our lieutenant heard about it
> and he says, "As soon as you see an Arvn pick up a weapon, first
> I want you to kill the lieutenant and then I want you to wipe out
> all his men . . . We continued to beat them up and nobody shot
> anybody.

Meantime, the VC/NVA imposed the ultimate passivity on
marines by making them the instruments of their own death.
For the VC/NVA were "good at skills that we didn't even
know — like booby traps." Most booby traps are arranged to
have the victim act as his own executioner. There is a
mockery involved which probably accounts for the term. It is
a trap for the booby. The only aggression permitted the
marine was against himself. The more aggressive the marine
tried to be, the more susceptible he was to booby traps.

Marines continued to be their own victims when they tried
to fight on the terms of the VC/NVA. The marines began
using a highly sophisticated mine called the Claymore that
they expected to be far more effective than the relatively crude
booby traps of the VC/NVA. The Claymore has pellets in the
front that are fired by an explosive in the back. However, the
VC/NVA were able to carry the Claymore one step further:

They can sneak right up and turn your Claymore around. And then you start moving around there so you'll hit the Claymore and it's turned around. You'll be the one that gets it.

Booby trapped by their own booby traps. As the marines sought a new means of becoming more aggressive, they were made still more passive.

The invisibility of the VC/NVA and the visibility of the marines were the underlying reasons for the success of one and the failure of the other with booby traps. For there are two conditions that must be met if a booby trap is to operate successfully. First, the hunter must know where his prey will be. Second, the prey must not know where the hunter has been.

There is an interval between planting and detonating a booby trap. The aggressor is removed in both time and space from his agression. But the marines (and the corner boys before them) were unaccustomed to aggression that was not spontaneous. This was another reason they had both a problem setting booby traps and a propensity for tripping them.

The ambush is closely related to the booby trap. It relies on one's own invisibility and the other's visibility. There are, in addition, the elaborate preparations that require deferred aggression. For these reasons, the ambushes prepared by the marines were subject to the same problems as the booby traps that they set:

Every night these NVA or VC used to come down and they used to screw up marine ambushes. And they always used to get away. They'd know where the ambush was set up and killer teams were set up. They'd sneak by them when they go into the village to get their rice and what they needed and leave. And then they'd screw them up on the way back. They'd fire on the ambush. And they'd take off up into the mountains. They did this every night. And they [marines] never got any of them.

Hiding entails actively seeking invisibility. It is ordinarily considered a passive act, because it is seen as the avoidance of action. More important, it is seen as the avoidance of being acted upon. But in the context of Vietnam, both these components were redefined when they became the means by which the VC/NVA were able to act aggressively. To speak of a means and end suggests a distinction, but none was easily made here. Instead, the means and end were part of the same process. When the VC/NVA hid, it was not only a way to avoid disadvantageous encounters with the marines, it was preparation for engaging the marines on advantageous terms:

> A lot of times you don't see them. A lot of times doesn't anybody ever see them I would think. They suck you into some type of ambush situation where there's a lot of them and a lot of yous. And they've already preregistered the area. Like two weeks before that they'll lie in the same position and fire their weapons for effect.

The means was not entirely passive because it was part of an aggressive end and the end was not entirely aggressive because it was part of a passive means. That is, the VC/NVA strategy was all the more difficult for the marines to sort out because it was cyclical. The marines found that the VC/NVA "aren't staying and fighting." Instead, "they hit you and run." But the running could not be classified as passive, because in addition to being the last stage of an aggressive act, it was the first stage of the next aggressive act.

The confusion that resulted from trying to classify the tactics of the VC/NVA is reflected in the following account where the VC are shuttled between categories of defense and offense:

> Well see, the VC was more or less on a defense all the time. Always hiding and coming out at night. But he still had to move around, unless he was in a large group. But he always had to be

the aggressor. And he was always under cover and stuff. So when he did come out and you did get in contact with him, he was determined that either he was going to die or he was going to get one of us.

When the VC/NVA hid, it was an aggressive act even if it did not lead to an engagement with the marines. For the marines had an aggressive mission in Vietnam. They were there to eliminate the VC/NVA. A status quo meant failure. The objective of the Marine Corps was summed up by the name given their "search-and-destroy missions." The VC/NVA could thwart these missions by hiding:

You'd go in there for three days; you'd pull out. And if they were there anyways, they weren't there when we got there. I imagine they must have come back after we left. So those are the most useless operations I ever heard of. If they seen a hole they'd start saying, "Oh, I bet there's weapons down there. I bet there's rice down there." We'd dig it up and there'd be nothing there. We never found nothing. I went on three of those, never found nothing.

The only result of these operations would be "carrying a couple of dead guys back — our own," men who encountered booby traps.

Catching those who hide is a form of aggressiveness, except in Vietnam. The contradiction of being permitted by the enemy to take the initiative was described by a former marine: "You catch them when they want you to catch them. They have all their bunkers and everything all set for you."

Traditionally, setting the time and place of battle has been another aggressive characteristic. The marines found themselves helping to set these terms because the VC/NVA "just wait 'til I guess they think they have you at your weakest, then they hit you." Another veteran provides an illustration:

Usually they'll hit the areas that are most secure. The lines were never checked. There won't be much bother about falling

to sleep on watch. The platoon commander didn't care because
we were never hit. Everyone gets to not caring.

Here too the apparent passivity of the VC/NVA was the
means to — or, rather, part of — an aggressive act. For they
were able to make the camp vulnerable by not attacking it.

The marines had a sense of being objects that comes from
being continually visible while those viewing them remain for
the most part invisible. But they had not adapted to the
dangers that follow from this condition. It was only in retrospect that the marine veteran just quoted saw that the more
"secure" they felt, the less secure they were in fact. In Vietnam, when the VC/NVA abstained from an attack it was
regarded as security not as a forewarning. There was less
stress for the marines in undergoing an attack that was observ-
able than in admitting to themselves that they were living with
an unseen threat.

Telescoped examples of this dilemma could occur several
times a day to the same men. A former marine tells of
walking at the head of a patrol along a trail:

> You see a shell case. So you start to step over this way. But you
> think: "Maybe it was put there on purpose so I'd step over that
> way." So it really screws your head up. The hell with it. I'd
> step over this way. And if it blows, it'll blow.

The weakness of the marines was maximized by not only the
behavior but more particularly through the attitudes with
which they were provided by the VC/NVA.

The disadvantageous visibility of the marines was a joint
project of themselves and the VC/NVA. If both sides were
equally visible, the advantage would belong to the American
troops who outnumbered the VC/NVA. It is only because
the VC/NVA were invisible that they could capitalize on the
visibility of the marines. The invisibility of the VC/NVA
provided them with a safe view of marines as a prelude to safe

action against them: "They could be hiding under a rock, or in a tunnel. We could walk right over them so they could see everything you have. What the hell can you do? They're watching you all the time, you never see them."

All this means that the marines were less visible to themselves than they were to the VC/NVA. Until the marines set off a mine or walked into an ambush, they did not usually know where they were in relation to the VC/NVA. In one way or another, "You wait to get hit; wait for them to come to you." But there was more involved than the VC/NVA seeing precisely what dangers the marines were exposed to. For the VC/NVA saw into the operations of the marines, as well as the context in which they were held. It amounted to the marines having to rely on the VC/NVA in order to view themselves. The VC made this reliance explicit:

> They talk to us all the time and shit — loud-speakers. In fact they told us one night, before anyone that was with us knew it, that we were going to move up to Phu Bai. Imagine that! They told us over a loud-speaker that they were pulling us out, because they knew if we stayed there that the VC were going to anni-hilate us. They said, "They're going to send you up to Phu Bai, let you rest for a while." So the squad leader went to the CO and they checked on it and we were going to move out about three weeks later. So they knew it before we did. That kind of fucked up your mind a little, you know.

(The announcement by the VC was in English — which was a way of telling the marines that their language, too, was visible.)

Even a formal statement of defeat by the VC/NVA could be made into an aggressive act by them:

> One day eight [NVA] turned themselves in. You could see their white flag. They had me walking up. I felt like an asshole. They're fucking clean. New uniforms. Spotless. Their boots

were shined. Haircuts. And they're supposed to be living in the mud? They're doing better than we are. And they're walking up. They're clean as a whistle. They had tailored uniforms. So everyone's there wondering: What's going on out there?

In describing the episode, this former marine wonders if "They just sent them out there to turn themselves in to make us look like they were doing good out there." But he dismisses this possibility. It is a reassuring one insofar as it indicates the prisoners were not typical. Yet, to accept this explanation would be an acknowledgement that the NVA were capable of deliberately redefining the terms of war by turning surrender on its head. Further, it would mean that the marines had accommodated this stratagem of the NVA.

Where the marines did succeed in killing, they often discovered that this could not be considered a form of domination, particularly when the victims were civilians. These deaths were both a cause and effect of the marines' passivity. For killing civilians usually meant the marines had lost control. The particular kind of control varied, but every case included a loss of control over the VC/NVA. When the marines were acting in rage, the civilians they killed served as surrogates for elusive VC/NVA. They were acting spontaneously at the time, but afterwards the marines saw their action as a loss of control over themselves:

> You see a guy you're really tight with for a period of months getting killed. We got really pissed off about it. You don't just say, "Well, fuck it." You go like kind of nutty. Anybody that even looked at you the wrong way you'd probably shoot. I think the American fighting man can be the most vicious ever. People don't realize this.

When civilians were killed through mistaken identity, it was a more direct reminder that the VC/NVA were beyond control, to the point of being unidentifiable. The misplaced aggressiveness of these acts sometimes resulted in ridicule, as when a marine shot what turned out to be a village elder one night and was afterwards nicknamed "Killer" by his fellow marines. His death was the outcome of a curfew rule that required the shooting of any violators. The curfew was imposed as a means of assuring that the VC/NVA would be identifiable.

Whatever the circumstances, killing civilians weakened the position of the marines. For it meant the villagers became still more dedicated to the VC/NVA, as seen in the following episode about the death of another elder:

> There's a killer team out one night. They were outside this village. This old man, he was a villager, was going out to do a crap in the rice paddy. And he was killed. That was right at the edge of the village. He was mistaken for a VC. Immediately after that happened the villagers turned VC sympathizers. After that there was always a build up of VC coming in. Along Highway 1, on the other side of the village, it was always mined. After this happened there was like a triple amount of mines planted in the road. And there was a road going up to the top of the hill. It was never really combed for any mines. Two days later a jeep went over a mine and blew up. That never happened before. But I imagine it was the villagers.

There were other ways in which the marines discovered that killing might not, after all, be the ultimate measurement of domination. For example, the VC/NVA were seen controlling to a point where they did not always consider killing necessary. This realization about the VC/NVA added to their control over the marines:

> This [NVA] goes, "Good morning, marines." A lot of shit they did just to fuck up your head. I mean, they must have had chances before that to really fucking zap someone. They did this shit just to fucking scare the fuck out of you. Just to let you

know that they were on the ball and they weren't fucking
around. Everyone fucking flies out on the trenches with their
rifles. They're expecting attack. Fucking gook is probably
laughing his ass off in the bushes.

Earlier, hiding was recognized as a means of killing. But here
it was seen as a more subtle form of aggression — a means
of killing morale. The marines were as unable to cope with this
sophisticated approach as with the VC/NVAs' apparently
unsophisticated agrarian approach to combat.

The disorientation of the marines was magnified by their
discovery that more than themselves was being relegated to
passivity. The same thing was happening to the previously
inviolate technology that had permitted the United States to
maintain an aggressive stance in the world. Here too the
victim brought on his own undoing. For the aggressiveness of
this technology in Vietnam was often self-destructive. The
following episode is typical of what could happen when technological superiority was invoked instead of dealing with the
VC/NVA on equal terms:

Say you had 30 gooks in the open. And you were too far away
from them. Instead of losing men over them, artillery was the
best bet. But we had so many restrictions on us. Like when we
had to call an artillery mission. They had to get air clearance
which is make sure there wasn't any helicopters flying around in
the area or any jet, any phantoms, flying over the area. So by
the time we got that clearance then we'd have to get a ground
clearance making sure that there wasn't any friendly troops
around that area. So by the time the clearance came in, they
were walking away. I mean they were just gone.

This failure had much to do with the characteristics of
technology that were taken for granted when they appeared in
the United States. Its massiveness was conspicuously inappropriate for the intimacy of combat in Vietnam where no one

group was at a great distance from any other group. The bureaucracy attached to the technology was intended to make it manageable, but in the fluidity of this combat the bureaucracy made it all the more unmanageable.

When the technology did the managing, its usefulness was cancelled out. Even where it protected some troops, its overabundance made others more vulnerable:

> One time we got sent in with Army guys, an Army artillery outfit. They've got all this logistical support. They've got hundreds of guys. They've got tanks — two crews. A night crew and a day crew. They really had it good. And they run over one of our guys. We were on a red alert. We were supposed to get hit for about a week. We were like supposed to be surrounded. And we were sleeping outside. They were moving in on us. So this track vehicle come up and rolled over two of our guys. And crushed one of their heads in. And run the other one across here and he died. And it was like a steel tread vehicle — ammo carrier.

It was even more difficult for technology than for marines to differentiate between friend and enemy.

Moreover, the futility of technology was carefully engineered by the VC/NVA. They were skilled at bringing out its limitations. Just as they made the visibility of marines a disadvantage by emphasizing the opposite characteristic among themselves, so they were able to turn technology into a disadvantage by not trying to fight it with technology. Again they stressed an opposite; this time, nature. It was a matter of building a strategy out of both their strength and the marines' weakness. Americans were unaccustomed to nature being used aggressively. When necessary, the land was used as a weapon:

> Like valleys where you're pinned down. A lot of times we've had jets come in over the top of us, when it was hard to hit them any

other way. They couldn't come across because of the mountains and stuff. They release the bombs right over our heads. And you can see the bombs. They'd be going towards us. And we're saying, "Ooh, fucking things just don't drop." But they like carried on the momentum of the speed they're going. They go in front of you. They blow up. That takes a lot of skill on an estimate. And a lot of fucking luck. The gooks choose this type of thing because they know that our jets can't come into a valley this way and make it. Because there's a mountain there and they can't get up. So they set up their defenses so they can shoot down the planes as they're coming in.

The rationale for much of American technology had been the conquest of nature. But in Vietnam, the VC/NVA used nature for the conquest of technology.

Technological futility led to occasional attempts at de-emphasizing technology. But this only made way for problems that were more subtle and therefore less predictable, for it brought out the other levels on which American culture was not transferable. To be more exact, these problems were subtle to the Americans, but they were glaring to everyone else. A program was established to work with the villagers in a manner that minimized technology:

We had an outfit that was called CAC — Combined Action Company. But cac in Vietnamese means prick. So they had to change it to Combined Action Platoons. They called it CAP. . . . It was a laughing stock of the villages. And the VC played it to the hilt.

The extent to which the ethos of this war disoriented the marines was reflected in their way of trying to cope with it. For they engaged in a classification of the VC/NVA that was in itself disorienting. While the Arvn represented what the marines feared they were becoming, the VC/NVA represented what the marines would like to have been. It was typically thought that in contrast to the Arvn, the VC "have a lot of balls." When inapplicable, such metaphors of courage assisted in linking cowardice to a lack of masculinity — which is a short conceptual distance from homosexuality.

Through relating to the VC/NVA, the marines were seeking a way to offset their inability to relate to the terms of the War. Their approval of the VC/NVA was reflected in the narrative of a former marine whose unit had suffered heavy casualties on several occasions, so that it was known as "The Walking Dead." Eventually they found themselves at Khe Sanh. The NVA had them surrounded and were again inflicting substantial damage without being damaged. The siege was so thorough that the NVA were tunneling underneath the marine positions. During the excavation, a marine used a stethoscopic device to overhear the conversation of the NVA digging below:

> Scared as everybody was, you had to fucking laugh hearing them swearing and shit. 'Cause they were like us really. I figured the [NVA] grunts were there exactly like us. They didn't like the fucking shit more than we did. They're probably down there swearing about their fucking officers and fucking shit like that. It was funny. We were really laughing.

There was another way in which the marines benefited from thinking of the VC/NVA in personal terms. It made the VC/NVA visible — only to a slight degree, but it was that much of an improvement over invisibility. The contrasting visibility of the marines was demonstrated when "they'd shoot at you at midnight. You'd light up a smoke and then he'd shoot at you." The unseen sniper was made visible insofar as he received a name from the marines: "Bed-Check Charley."

While the personalization of the VC/NVA operated in a way that provided positive feelings, the impersonalization of the VC/NVA was invoked to prevent negative feelings. The

fact that the NVA were trying to kill marines was explained
away by one former marine who recalled that "you don't dis-
like them, because no one NVA ever did anything to you."

In other words, the marines did not suppose that the
VC/NVA, on such occasions, were acting personally toward
them. Clearly, the same could not be said about the Arvn.
The marines had no trouble relating specific grievances to
specific Arvn. Moreover, they had a sense that homosexuality
was more personal than death.

# CHAPTER IV

# Flashbacks

MARINES RETURNING HOME are sometimes preceded by this letter sent to their families:

### HEADQUARTERS

FROM:   Rehabilitation Office
TO:
SUBJECT:   Vietnam veteran attempted rehabilitation of

Having completed his tour of duty in the Far East, ———— is being permitted to return to the land of the big PX for attempted rehabilitation. Please keep in mind that your Marine has, in all probability, been subjected to severe psychological trauma, Asiatoons fenations, rice paddy fever, Viet Congitis, and too much Kool-Aid. In making joyous preparations to welcome him back home, you must allow for the crude environment in which he has existed for the last year.

For both your convenience and safety, the following set of guidelines has been prepared. Strict compliance with them is highly recommended for your peace of mind and well-being.

A. Show no alarm if he is not housebroken for the first ten days.
B. If he complains of sleeping in a room without a mosquito net,

humor him with a net and a few mosquitoes to lull him to sleep.

C. Show reverance when he mentions coupon photos or Baby Jane.

D. Be understanding when he insists on building a machine gun bunker in the front yard.

E. Don't attempt to stop him when he walks around fully armed, and encourages others to do the same.

F. Don't be surprised when he starts a neighborhood Pacification Program, or even organizes the clowns who didn't make the romantic trip to the Far East into groups digging foxholes, filling sandbags, or making night patrols.

### TAKE THESE PRECAUTIONS

A. Shock may be caused by the sight of a beautiful woman, people laughing and dancing, television, or the sight of a foamy head of beer.

B. Don't let him associate with mixed groups until his profanity decreases and his English is back to normal.

C. Get your women off the street, hide the corn liquor, and put a lock on the refrigerator.

### PAY NO ATTENTION WHEN

A. He mixes snails with his rice, or pours catsup on his food to make it taste better.

B. He sits squat-legged on the floor.

C. He drinks milk out of a bowl, or uses two forks to cut his meat.

### SAY NOTHING WHEN

A. He stares at chairs, or a soft mattress.

B. He talks to himself when alone in a room.

C. He mumbles in Vietnamese to anyone he doesn't feel like speaking English to.

DO NOT — I REPEAT, DO NOT ASK

A. Does it rain in Viet Nam?
B. Are the women in Da Nang really flat chested?
C. How was the mail service?
D. How was liberty in Da Nang?

BE TOLERANT WHEN HE

A. Pads around the house, clad only in sandals and a towel.
B. Slyly offers to sell cigarettes to the postman.
C. Picks suspiciously at his food as though you were trying to poison him.

BUT ABOVE ALL

Keep in mind that beneath that tanned and rugged exterior there is a heart of gold (the only thing of value he has left). Treat him with love, kindness, tolerance, and an occasional fifth of good liquor (Boondock Bourbon will not do!). With luck you will soon be able to rehabilitate that which once was (but now is the hollow shell of) the happy-go-lucky guy you once knew and loved.

by direction,

Heele B. Homesoon
Major   USMC

There is no "Rehabilitation Office" in the Marine Corps. In one sense, the letter is an invention. The returning marine sends it himself. One veteran explained, "It's pretty funny over there. But when you come back you find yourself doing some of those things."

As the mocking seriousness — or serious mocking — of this letter suggests, there is a variety of ways in which Vietnam reappears in the life of veterans. "Flashbacks" are how they sometimes describe the most prevalent and persistent of the reappearances. It refers to those instances when they believe themselves in Vietnam. In their mildest form, flashbacks occur so fleetingly that veterans have no opportunity to react to them. At the other extreme, veterans react with violence. The flashbacks occur in a wide range of shapes and sizes. The flashbacks that cause violence last from a few seconds to a few hours. They usually last a few minutes. There can be a single flashback or a sequence of them — each alternating with reality. The occasions on which flashbacks occur are likely to be less frequent over time. However, the intensity does not diminish — at least over the three-year period of observation. The most violent episodes generally occurred when veterans had been home for at least six months.

The theme running through the immeidate causes of flashbacks is a sense of danger. This danger is usually seen only by the veteran. The father of a veteran recalls that he was watching television one night when his son came out of another room and attacked him. Other members of the family tried to restrain the veteran who "kept saying, 'I won't talk, you gooks. I won't talk.'" It was clear to his mother that "he was screaming like these were his enemies." But neither she nor anyone else present had any idea of what caused the flashback. As for the veteran himself, "I don't remember doing anything that they said I did."

However, the cues for flashbacks are not always obscure. Three veterans were enrolled in a special program at a university where they were sitting in a dormitory room one evening when a firecracker exploded outside the door. Each veteran suddenly returned to Vietnam. One dove under a bed and another began firing a toy gun. The third veteran recalls, "I was thinking I was back in the fucking 'Nam." He grabbed the pipe from a towel rack and attacked the student he thought was responsible for the explosion.

On an earlier occasion this same veteran found himself

backed against a wall during a fight in his neighborhood. He discussed his feelings of being "encircled" in much the same way he had once described the time in Vietnam when "we got it from both sides" and "took 75 per cent casualties." In this case, however, he was encircled by one person and stabbed him several times with a knife.

Because this violence is beyond the control of veterans, it also has the characteristic of turning them into spectators. They fear an adversary less than what they see themselves doing — more accurately, what they see themselves having done. After attacking the student, the veteran recalls, "I was scared. Not because I was afraid. But because of what I did." In these after-the-fact appraisals, it often becomes clear that the spectator is in a real sense the civilian that he was before joining the service. When he reflected on his knifing the opponent who encircled him, the veteran concluded, "That's not like me. 'Cause I never used to do anything like that." The "me" to which he refers is the prewar civilian. At the same time, the combatant component of himself is described in the second person: "The only way for you to react to that in the 'Nam is to kill the people who threaten you." The confusion of selves appeared in his account of a time when he and another veteran were fighting an opponent: "I went in the house and got the two big butcher knives. I gave him one and I gave me — I, I took one." Midway through a different fight he shifted from the combatant to the civilian when "I realized: I'm going to kill the fucking guy. So I stopped and I went at him with my fists."

Even more distressing to the veterans is that when they observe their violence retrospectively it must often be through the eyes of others, for they are likely to have little or no recollection of the episodes. This was the case with a veteran whose parents were usually the victims of his violence. He knew from what they afterwards told him he was saying and

doing that on one level he had been reliving particularly
threatening experiences from Vietnam. Every time this relapse
occurred:

> I was scared of myself. Because when my father or mother
> would tell me these things, I was afraid that now what if I kill
> somebody? What am I going to do? I can't say to a cop: "I
> don't know. I don't know what I did." What am I going to do?
> I don't know.

For their part, family members also have a limited view of
the violence. They have little or no basis for understanding
the cause of an episode. Even where it is obvious to them that
a veteran is undergoing a flashback to Vietnam, they are likely
to be uninformed about the Vietnam experience that gave rise
to the flashback. In most cases the veteran did not write home
about his more harrowing experiences, and once home does
not discuss them. The usual reason for keeping these experiences private is a feeling they cannot be shared. It is assumed
that only those who had undergone these experiences could
understand them. This assumption compounds the inability of
the relatives to understand.

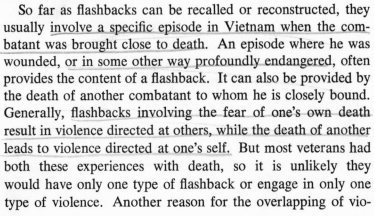

So far as flashbacks can be recalled or reconstructed, they
usually involve a specific episode in Vietnam when the combatant was brought close to death. An episode where he was
wounded, or in some other way profoundly endangered, often
provides the content of a flashback. It can also be provided by
the death of another combatant to whom he is closely bound.
Generally, flashbacks involving the fear of one's own death
result in violence directed at others, while the death of another
leads to violence directed at one's self. But most veterans had
both these experiences with death, so it is unlikely they
would have only one type of flashback or engage in only one
type of violence. Another reason for the overlapping of vio-

lence is that veterans frequently harm themselves in an effort to avoid harming others.

It is no accident that veterans have selected a movie term, flashback, to describe the revisits of their minds to Vietnam. The frame of reference provided by films comes closer than any other to helping the veterans understand and describe the nature of their violence. The term sums up the detachment of veterans from the part of themselves that remains a combatant. Since films are the product of others, they are viewed. The spectators are not responsible for the images they view.

Further, the violence of veterans is unreal to themselves insofar as it is incomprehensible. They often refer to their actions as "weird," but this unreality is more vivid than their usual activities. In the same way, movies are able to present unreality so that it is more vivid than reality. Such movie scenes are larger than life, though not lifelike.

Flashbacks also have much in common with the recurring dreams of these veterans. They dream about encounters with death in Vietnam. While the dreams are unreal to the extent they defy time and space, they too impinge on reality — in this case by remaining in their waking thoughts. Yet, whether a flashback or a dream is involved, the veterans cannot usually recall more than fragments of the way in which they have reexperienced Vietnam. They have as little control over flashbacks as they do over dreams. Both illustrate the combat between past and present that is going on deeply within themselves.

For the same reason the Vietnam War is unique, its veterans are unique. Because it is a guerrilla war, it is different in kind from the other wars that Americans have fought since their Revolution. Up to a point, however, it does share characteristics with other wars. No combat situation has ever allowed a lowering of defenses. But in Vietnam any situation

was potentially a combat one. American combatants learned
to continually expect danger in unexpected places. Similarly,
veterans are in a continual state of alertness. A wife who
found herself the target of flashbacks remarked about her
husband: "Even sitting around, he can't seem to relax. He's
all tensed up." The continuity of vigilance between Vietnam
and home was expressed by a veteran who periodically saw his
brothers and parents as Viet Cong:

> When you're there [Vietnam], you're always wary of things. You
> never know. You just don't understand. And when you think
> you hear something, you really don't. But I mean, maybe you
> do. Like when I go to bed at night, it takes me three hours to go
> to sleep. I don't want to get sleeping pills, because one of these
> nights I'm going to want to kill myself — take a whole bottle or
> something. If I go to bed and it's raining out or something, I
> don't go to sleep until it ends. And then I know I'm all right.
> And maybe I'll fall asleep. But I've stayed up until 6 o'clock in
> the morning waiting. Waiting for something to happen. 'Cause
> I expect it to happen.

This alertness to danger is readily translated into a response
to danger. A veteran who had attacked his mother and sister
on various occasions explained the incidents in terms of Vietnam where he learned to act on impulse:

> It's just like a fucking machine. It's the same thing when you
> come back from overseas. You're still a fucking machine. You
> act on impulse.

An additional machinelike characteristic results in part
from having experienced a routinization of death. According
to a different veteran:

> All over the place you see guys with legs blown off, gooks with
> their heads blown off and their chests wide open and all kinds of
> shit. You just say, "Man, is that all there is to it? Is that all
> there is to it?" Just, you're dead. And no more. And you get

that attitude that people are just matter. It's just something you begin to live with.

This routinization is part of the combatants' life in any war. But the guerrilla aspects of the Vietnam War imposed a sense of futility on American combatants that carried over to civilian life. When the veteran who began "to live with" death returned home, "I felt like I got screwed because I didn't get killed." Death had meaning insofar as it provided relief from futility. In time, he could not even make that argument for death:

> Now I know it was stupid to go over there in the first place. I don't know why they died. They died for nothing if you ask me. Because a guy dying on the ground that I was buried — I mean, I was stationed at, what did he accomplish?

This inadvertent reference to his own burial in Vietnam reflects a common view about the persistent futility of an unrequited war that has helped to keep combat experiences alive. The "nothing" they died for makes the death senseless. In Vietnam, the phrase frequently used for "killed" was "wasted." This senselessness meant that death was soon viewed without senses. Emotions died. As described by another veteran:

> Before, if anybody dies, I'd feel bad for a long time and talk about it. But now, when someone dies, you just say, "Well, that's life." One day, we got hit out on the perimeter and we lost some guys. At first I missed them. But when you see a couple more of it, it was just, "Well, too bad." There was no meaning after that. You felt bad, but there's no deep feeling about it. It makes you lose feeling.

"That's life" has as little meaning as death. By losing his feelings, he essentially lost himself. In referring to himself "before," he says "I." In referring to himself "now," he says "you." When the contrast is not before and after Vietnam, but rather between Vietnam and the present, the terms of reference shift. The veteran who feared sleeping at night and suicide used "you" when he meant himself in Vietnam and "I" when he meant himself at the present time.

While flashbacks arise as a means of avoiding dangers that are reminiscent of Vietnam, they often have the effect of imposing additional frustrations of guerrilla war. Again, there is a reliance on the "enemy" to understand the dangers of one's own position — when it comes to learning what happened during the flashback. Again, there is a danger to one's self from the spontaneity of one's own violence — whether this be through physical harm or through the legal penalty for harming others. Again, the targets are frequently those who are nominally on one's own side.

Further, the veteran finds that his readjustment becomes more difficult as he becomes more of a civilian. For to the extent he is a civilian, the veteran tends to look at his war experiences out of context. The incidents are still vivid, but the rationales often become less clear or less convincing. In other cases, there were no articulated rationales at the time. When they occurred, the actions seemed natural. But in retrospect, they begin to appear unnatural. When they seemed natural, it was because these actions were considered necessary. Whether it was a logistical necessity or an emotional necessity, combatants frequently acted before they could deliberate. There was no time to develop justifications. There were also occasions when they did not want to recognize their justifications. In any event, combatants referred to the United States as "the world" because they were beyond its constraints. To a considerable degree, the War was fought in a moral vacuum. No rationales were required. Here is how a veteran explained his previous reluctance to discuss episodes in Vietnam: "It's just — it was our company, our platoon. What we did in the villages were amongst ourselves."

As the punishment emerges more clearly than the crime, the term "vicious" is sometimes used by the veterans to describe their activities in Vietnam. It is one way that another type of after-the-fact appraisal is revealed. For the term rests on the sort of moral judgment that was inconsistent with the activity in the first place. These judgments are the work of the civilian component of the veteran; they are directed at his combatant component. Although the necessities of training and combat extinguished the civilian component, it tends to progressively reemerge after his homecoming. The accompanying increase of self-condemnation creates a growing tension between the two selves. It helps to make his war experiences live issues.

But Vietnam at least had the advantage of providing accessible targets to which blame could be attached. After returning home, the administration is often blamed. A distillation of this feeling was expressed by one of the veterans: "Fifty thousand Americans died, for what? For fucking political assholes." The inaccessibility of the administration multiplies the futility. Yet, it has been this remoteness that resulted in the administration being selected for blame in the first place. It is felt the administration escaped accountability for the War while veterans bore its stigmatizing effects.

The problem of readjustment is further compounded by the veteran's efforts to faciliate it. He soon discovers how little control he has over his own violence. Although the violence is infrequent and brief, the possibility of its occurring is constant. With the hope of minimizing provocations, the veteran tends to isolate himself. This withdrawal is most likely to occur when his tension builds up slowly enough to provide a forewarning. For gradual tension takes the form of "an urge you want to do something. Like you're sitting here [in a bar].

Sometimes you feel like splitting the table. And nobody
knows what you're doing. A lot of times you get up and you
walk away." This isolation helps to generate more of the
tension that induces violence. As he turns still further into
himself, there is a greater probability of his two selves con-
fronting each other.

The isolation is also imposed on the veteran by others. His
contemporaries who were not in Vietnam place veterans in a
separate category: "They're screwy. They're wary of everybody. [We] don't trust them." There is a widespread recognition that the traditional rules governing fights are not
observed by veterans:

> They have everything on their mind now. They seen people
> killed and they were killing over there. Everything's building
> up now. He'll have all these thoughts in his mind. You can
> see it in their eyes. And when someone picks a fight with them,
> the fucking guy will do anything: kill, stab. Anything. Like a
> fucking maniac. They just want to get their victim that they're
> fighting and kill.

A veteran who descirbed his own fights in much the same way
was contrasting them to his pre-Vietnam fights when "you
turned out to be the best of friends afterwards. Most likely I'd
help the guy up, shake hands with him, and say 'Let's have a
beer.' "

Even those who are closest to a veteran find themselves
placing him in the separate category. At the start of an argument, the friend of one veteran took an acquaintance aside at
a bar to explain that "he can kill someone fast. Don't press
him, please." In other cases, this sort of fear transcends
understanding and sympathy. A veteran left his wife after
attacking her. Although she knew about his dreams and
flashbacks, this did nothing to reduce her continual dread. As
she sat in the living room of their apartment and heard a noise

in the outside hall, she suddenly stopped speaking and became tense. She feared her husband had returned: "I'm scared half to death whenever I hear anyone out there."

Isolation has also been imposed by the government. The veteran has essentially been left to cope with his own readjustment. The military clearly recognizes the chasm between civilian life and combat, otherwise it would not have spent upwards of four months training the marine enlistee for Vietnam. The need for at least an equally elaborate program to assist the transition from combat to civilian life was overlooked by the government. A final example of self-destructive technology resulted from flying combatants home. Jet aircraft made it possible for them to become civilians, at least nominally, within a few days after leaving the jungle. Here is what the abrupt change meant to a veteran who had no police record before enlisting, but was charged with four assaults and batteries during the eighteen months since his homecoming:

> You're just different. You are. Not because you want to be. And then you come back. And within a matter of two to ten days you're supposed to be a human being again. You know, civilized. After living like an animal for so long. And right away you're supposed to come back and change. I couldn't do it.

The full effects of combat have not been recognized by any of the governmental agencies that could help to deal with them. The first phase of this denial occurred in Vietnam where, according to a former Army psychiatrist, "Every Army psychiatrist is paranoid." Specifically, "They're terrified of transfers. You get a feeling that one wants to do what daddy says because if one doesn't, he'll get transferred. And nobody likes to get transferred because one will always have the fantasy it will be to a worse place." Transfers resulted when a psychiatrist did "a very bad job in his division. By a 'bad job,' I mean according to the military." The military defini-

tion of a bad job was one that identified combat as the source
of a mental problem. A good job meant that "so many, many
of these kids who come in because of anxiety, for example,
might be called 'passive dependent characters' or 'passive
aggressive characters.' " As long as the diagnosis is a character problem, it is not classified as mental illness. There were
several reasons for the military wanting character problems to
be the diagnosis instead of the combat neuroses that were
acknowledged in World War II. By defining psychiatric
casualties out of existence, the administration could cite the
low psychiatric casualty rate of the Vietnam War. And since
a character disorder is defined as a condition that preceded
combat, the Veterans' Administration is not required to com-
pensate those alleged to suffer from it. Finally, men with
anxiety, for example, had to be evacuated. But they could
remain in combat with character disorders. "The basic philos-
ophy of psychiatric treatment in the Army in Vietnam,"
according to a document used at the U.S. Army Medical Field
Service School, is "first of all keep the individual at his job."

The Veterans' Administration is operated along lines that
do not require a readjustment to civilian life. In a typical
appraisal, one veteran observed that "they keep you running — it's just like the military." His comment was amplified
by another veteran:

> There's so much red tape, you lose a day's pay and then they tell
> you they can't see you 'til next Thursday. And then you go on
> Thursday and they say the doctor's not there.

In most instances, those veterans who do get to see profes-
sionals at the Veterans' Administration discover another way
in which it resembles the military. The Veterans' Administration is unwilling to acknowledge the emotional relevance of
combat in Vietnam. This unwillingness was reflected in a
memorandum from the Veterans' Administration in Washing-

ton, D.C., to directors of its various hospitals. A difference between the Vietnam veteran and veterans of other wars was acknowledged insofar as: "He is less willing to accept authority in a compliant manner." But this meant that he was no different from nonveterans his age:

> It should be recognized that this characteristic of today's veteran is shared with youth in general. Even such strongholds of authority as football coaches have remarked that players no longer accept training rules and practice routines automatically.

Now my brother won't trust me at all. He won't even let me hold his kids when I go up to the house. I'm a godfather of one of them, and I can't hold it. I don't even ask to hold the kid when he's there. 'Cause one time when I asked to hold the kid he was drinking a few beers and he said, "Don't let that fucking nut near the kid."

There's eleven kids in the family. My mother's an alcoholic. I come home one day. And I wasn't drinking. I just walked in. And it just hit me. The kids were all mulling around or something. And my mother was drunk.

I said, "What did you have to eat?" Or something like that.

And they said they didn't eat. It was about six o'clock at night.

And I said, "You didn't eat?"

They said, "No."

And one of the kids asked me if he could make a sandwich. He asked *me* if he could make a sandwich.

I said, "It's there, eat it."

I said something to my mother about, "Why don't you feed
the kids?" And she said something to me.

And all of a sudden: Boom! I didn't even know where I
was.

And the next thing I knew is that I woke up. I was on the
floor when I woke up.

They said I was saying, "I'm not. No, I'm not," or shit like
that; mumbling, you know.

They said I was trying to kill her. I was strangling her. It
took my uncle and my father and my two brothers to take me
from her. And if they weren't there, I would have killed her.

And I don't even remember it. All I remember was that
when I woke up I was on the kitchen floor. And they said I
was there for a good five minutes on the floor. And I just
don't remember how it happened, or what I did. When they
told me that I was strangling her, I don't remember it. And I
told them all, they're full of shit. And they said that's what I
was doing.

My father said that I thought it was some Vietnamese
broad.

And the only thing I can remember like it in Vietnam was
that I kicked the shit out of this one Vietnamese broad, because she had a grenade in her blouse. We were searching
these people in a village. We were just searching them down.
And we found this one broad with a grenade stuffed in between
her boobs. I almost killed her. Because I seen one of my buddies blown up. It's not a good sight. And this broad is thinking the same thing. So I beat the shit out of her.

They said I was saying shit like, "You little bitch."

I don't remember. I don't remember doing it to my mother,
you know. I don't know what happened in that space of time.
And when I woke up they told me. Because I couldn't say
why I did it. If I did know, I'd be all right.

I went over to the VA because I was scared. And when I

seen the doctor and I told him about it, he told me it was my nerves.

"Keep it cool. Take these pills."

He gave me some white pills with a red stripe around them and some other little, tiny pills that look like malaria pills.

He said, "Take these and you'll be all right."

I started taking the pills: I'd get all dopey. I'd walk into the wall, for Christ's sake, trying to get from here to the kitchen. So I quit taking the pills.

I drive down to my father-in-law's house. And all I remember is getting out of the car. I don't really remember going into the house.

So then they told me that first I started hitting him with a belt. And he ran upstairs to avoid me and I ran up after him. And he went in the bedroom and I kicked the door so hard that actually the wood just, you know, there's a hole in the door like this now. Then he ran into the bathroom. And I kicked that door through and went in there and like we started to wrestle, I guess. The bathroom bowl somehow ended up off completely.

And then — I most remember this now that we're talking about it — as we started fighting, he got on top of me. I remember he had me down, I don't think I could move him. So I just took a good bite out of his eyebrow. I wasn't aiming for the eyebrow or nothing. I took a few bites out of, like the chest. And when I seen his face, I just grabbed his head and pulled it down and took a good bite out of it. Then he ran out of the house.

And then they came in. And I didn't say nothing. My mother-in-law looked and seen blood like on the table, here and there. And I was all covered with blood. They told me he went out and got the cops and went to a hospital. He had to get stitches.

It's starting to come back more and more now. I never talked about it before. Never thought of it. I still don't remember going into the house. I don't remember hitting him with the belt. I don't remember anything happened downstairs; just upstairs.

Like I feel myself now kicking the door. The first door — the bedroom door. But I can't remember being in the bathroom, though. But surely we must, because the bowl was all screwed up. And I remember, I can feel, I can remember myself biting him. I remember when they came in, I still felt the urge to kill him.

Like, "What happened?"

I said, "I don't know."

"What did you fight about?"

"I don't know."

But I still knew I was going to kill him the second he come back in.

It's come back a lot, but I still can't remember going into that house and having — I guess maybe we had words or something. I don't know. All they said was I tore off my belt and started hitting him with the belt. And I guess the two brothers ran out, 'cause they thought I was going crazy or something.

I don't actually remember being in the bathroom. But I remember just grabbing his head like this, just pulling it down. I remember tasting the hair off the eyebrow and like just spitting it out. And then, I guess, I must have just got up and run downstairs.

I can remember: "I'm going to kill him, I'm going to kill him." But why? I don't know why.

I felt bad. Really bad. I don't even remember if I slept that night or not. How the Christ could I ever bite the guy in the eyebrow?

When he came back from Vietnam, it was just little things I noticed.

We were sitting down eating dinner and an airplane would go by and this terrible look would come on his face. But I said to myself, "Well, these things are to be expected."

And at night time he'd be asleep and he'd wake up and he'd start screaming off about something. One night it was, "Shut off the red light, Charley's going to see it." It's mostly mumbling. But you know it's about Vietnam.

Everything was going fine and it all really started. He was home and he was so short-tempered. M always had a bad temper, but this was a ridiculous kind of a temper where he would really go into such a rage that, God, he'd kill anybody.

Evidently I kept all my anger inside me, because every time he slashed out at me — you know, "there's dust on the floor," or he'd pick me up on anything and really go into a rage about it. I mean small things like "the potatoes are not done right," and really go into a big rage about something like that.

And of course I said to myself, "Well, I'm not going to argue with him." So I was going to be very quiet, which was wrong on my part for myself. I was keeping all my anger in, until finally I had it up to here.

And that's when I had a breakdown. It was a weird thing. They said it was an emotional breakdown caused by anxiety. So they put me in the Medical Center Hospital. And it took them a long time for me to stop from getting those attacks. All these horrible feelings were going through me. And they were trying all different medications on me and nothing would calm me down. I was just plain hysterical.

When I was finally released, the day I was released, I went down to talk to the psychiatrist and they said, "Your husband is in the VA hospital."

And I looked at them.

He said he was outside the hospital. He wanted to shoot Dr. A, which would mean one of my doctors, and Dr. B. They found him sitting outside the Medical Center in a car with a gun waiting to kill these two doctors.

I guess he thought maybe they weren't doing the right thing for me. They wanted to abort me. You know I was carrying N. All these psychiatrists claimed that I shouldn't carry her. M didn't want the abortion.

And of course they were mixing me up. They were playing with my mind, so that I was believing them. They said more or less, "You have this baby you're never going to be all right. You're going to crack up completely. See, you need that abortion and M has to sign those papers."

And M refused to sign them, but they were going to go ahead and do it anyway.

So M felt, "They're going to take my baby away, I'm going to kill them."

And from there they just took him to the VA hospital.

So I went to visit him and a priest was with me, Father C. And we were sitting in the rec room there, and M just kept on looking at me. And the next thing I knew he just picked up everything and he just started smashing — he went after both the priest and myself. He picked up their stereo. He wanted to kill us.

He said he was going to kill us. He was rambling on about Vietnam. I remember when they were taking him away it was something about "gooks." Everybody came running in to tell me to get out.

But I said, "Leave me alone. I want to calm him down." Because I thought I was the only one that could calm him down, being his wife and knowing him as well as I did. But the nurses dragged me out.

And I see these four big, big men come and take him. And that upset me very much, and I was screaming, "I can take care of him."

And they said, "No, not this time, Mrs. M, not this time."

And then the social worker came up and said "We don't want you to visit him anymore until we call you."

And that was about two months. And every time I called they wouldn't tell me anything.

Well, M escaped from the hospital. And the first thing they did was call the Medical Center when they found he was gone, figuring he's going to go out to kill these doctors. So the VA called me. Dr. D, that was her name, she called me and she said, "Mrs. M, you have to get your husband back there." You have to do this and you have to do that.

She said, "He's drugged up now, but once that wears off he may kill anybody."

And we were looking all over Boston for him. And then I went up to his mother's house. And he comes walking in with this silly old grin on his face like the little bad boy who ran away from home or something.

And I just said to him, "What are you doing?"

He says, "I decided to leave. There's nothing wrong with me."

There was no way I could get him to go back.

So Dr. D kept on calling, "You have to get him back, you have to get him back."

And I said, "Listen, he's a hundred ninety-five pounds, and I'm only ninety-five pounds. I can't just pick him up and carry him over."

*This* is when they wanted me. They didn't want anything to

do with me when he was there, but when he escaped they were constantly calling me, you know, "Do this."

So the only thing I could think of was go to Father C. So I went down to the rectory and Father C was just coming back from five o'clock mass.

And he says, "Did you find M?"

And I said, "Yes, he's at his mother's house. But," I says "he won't go back."

He says, "Let's drive down."

Father C made an agreement with M. M said he left because they wouldn't give him a weekend pass like they were giving the other men. And M wasn't about to go back unless he could get a weekend pass. You know, to leave for the weekend and then come back. And Father C said, "Okay, I'll go over there and I'll tell the doctor that. And if he says 'No,' I'll take you back."

And M went over there under those circumstances.

So this other doctor that was on, a very brilliant man, we went into the room, Father C, M, myself, and the doctor.

And Father C said, "I'm here as a priest and as a friend. I promised this man this, and I have to keep the promise that if you don't give him a weekend pass, I'm going to take him back out of this hospital."

And the doctor said, "I don't care who you are."

Then M and the doctor started arguing, and then M was practically in tears, "Why won't you let me out of here?"

And I'll never forget the way the doctor said, "M, once you learn how to use this [pointing to his mouth] instead of this [showing his fist], I'll let you out. Until then you're going to stay here until you rot."

They finally agreed to let me visit him. And when I did, it wasn't the same person I knew. He was constantly a nervous wreck. Just a complete nervous wreck. And if you knew M before Vietnam, he was the Rock of Gibraltar. Gee, nothing

could faze him, before Vietnam. I knew they were giving him
Stelazine and Thorazine and all sorts of things. But it wasn't
helping.

And they finally agreed to a day pass with me, if I took him
out to a hockey game or something, but I had to have him
back at a certain time.

And it was a big responsibility. Because we'd be in a sub-
way station and he'd be like he was looking for something, or
waiting for something to happen. He was a nervous wreck.
And the hockey game, I don't even think he watched it. Like
he was waiting for somebody to attack him, jump on him.

And he was like that all the time we went to visit him at the
hospital. And then he escaped again. And when he did, he
refused to go back.

And the doctors called me, and I said, "Listen I've talked to
him, the priest has talked to him, everybody. There's no way
he is going back."

We'd get into these little spats where he'd just went, oh god,
a complete rage. You know, start breaking furniture and
everything like that. Anything in sight he'll pick up and start
throwing at you — anything. He doesn't care what it is. And
screaming. "I'm going to kill you, I'm going to kill you."

And I just kept my cool until one night. He took such a
temper tantrum that he keeled over and he was holding his
heart. And he couldn't breath. And I called the VA clinic
and I told the doctor, and he said, "Well tell M to come over."

At that time they had him on an out-patient basis. And
they gave him — now this got me very upset — they gave him
Dilantin. They use them for people who take convulsions,
epileptics, anything of that nature. They gave these to M, and
they told him to take them.

Well, this was on a Saturday. So Sunday I gave M one, and
oh my god did he ever get sick.

And I said, "Well, come on, you have to go to the hospital."

I couldn't move him, nothing. So I said, "Well I'll call up
Dr. E." He's nowhere to be found. He's never in the phone
book. I called the VA.

"What should I do? I can't even get him into a cab." He
was just like dead, a rock. I couldn't lift him up or nothing.

He's going, "I'm dying. What the hell did you give me?"

And they said, "Well, if it gets any worse call us back."

I says, "How worse can it get? He may die."

But this is it. They didn't care.

☆   ☆   ☆

We did a number once on Commonwealth Ave. with this
faggot. Now I get in these moods where — like when I was in
'Nam, we'd walk through a village: you are a conqueror.
That's the way you felt. Whether you like it or not, that's the
way you felt.

And if you told a broad: "Lay down. You're going to get
laid," she's going to get laid. It's as simple as that. You don't
even have to pay her for it.

And if you want to kick the shit out of some Vietnamese
kid that's giving you a little mouth — kick the shit out of him.
Who's going to do anything? Nobody. Not even your
buddies. They just sit there and eat their chow, or whatever
they're doing.

And you feel vicious, you know. Like, I don't know.
These stories you read about what the Chinese do — before
you go to 'Nam you see these war pictures where all these guys
rape this one broad in the village. You think of that when
you're in 'Nam. Now there's no doubt about it, because I did.
And like it was amusing, you know.

And now when I got into the habit there, when I come
back, this place is no different. It seems like it's no different,
except there was in the jungle.

Now when I was over on Commonwealth Ave., we took this faggot. When you're in 'Nam everything had to be precise and on time. If you made a mistake you just might not live to regret it. So when I was on Commonwealth Ave., it's like the same thing. Like the car was up there and I look back at my buddy and I said, "Look it. I'm going to go in and I'm going to ask the guy is he going out. And if he says 'Yeah,' that means that everything's cool. I'll just hop in the car. And when I hop in the car, I shut the door; you come around at the same time on the driver's side so he can't get out. And when I shut the door, I'm going to hit him at the same time."

When I opened the door I said, "Hey, you going out?"

The guy says, "Yeah."

I said, "That's cool."

And I was thinking everything precise, just like in 'Nam. Like right there, that's it. And when I shut the door, it was a reaction like I did it all my life. And I never used to do this. Not until I needed the money.

And when I shut the door, just as I shut the door, I gave him a hooker. And I split his lip, and his nose was bleeding. And he was trying to get out. And my buddy came in the wrong door.

Now I got so mad at him, because if the cops come or something, we're done for. I think there's some law about punching out faggots, I don't know what it is. But he didn't even have to be a faggot. You just got an assault and battery charge right there, plus attempted robbery and all that shit.

So I'm grabbing him; pulling him in. And so my friend grabs him by the shirt; gets him in. And I told him to shut the door. He shut the door.

And I felt like a conqueror again, you know. I had him right where I wanted him.

And I felt like it was the same thing in 'Nam. If I wanted a broad I had one. If I wanted a mamasan to do my clothes, she did it. 'Cause if she didn't, I'd fucking shoot her. If I got mad enough, I'd shoot her. I'd shoot someone. And when you've got that weapon in your hands, you are the master. There's no two ways about it.

And a lot of times nobody cares. Your buddies — not even your officers give a shit. They call you by your first name. I used to call my lieutenant by his first name. And if someone gave me a hard time when I was in 'Nam, just give them a gun butt in the mouth. It'd straighten them out. Sure.

Like you couldn't take anything easy. You couldn't give an inch without them taking a whole yard. Because they'll steal every fucking thing you own and screw into the jungle. And you never see them again. You had to be a mean mother-fucker to survive there.

So when I was in that car with that guy, like my friend was telling me, "Fuck it." I only found six dollars on the guy.

I said, "Fuck this. This guy's got to have more than that."

And when I looked at him, I felt like taking him and punching his fucking roof in.

Like, "You better give me your fucking money. I'm demanding it."

If I had a gun I might have shot him, if he didn't do what I said. I had this comb. A long one with a pointed end on it. And I was taking it and I was stabbling him in the side with it. There was one friend sitting beside me and one in the back.

And they were telling me, "Slow down. Stop it." 'Cause I might fucking put it right through him. And I didn't realize what I was really doing until they told me.

All we got was six dollars, and my buddy turned around and gave him a dollar for gas — for chrissakes. That's after he drove us back. We made him drive us back. And when I left him, I gave him another punch in the face.

It was like, I don't know. I didn' mean to really stick him. But they said I was really jabbing it into him. And I didn't remember it. It was just like another space of time that I lost. And I felt, if I wanted to put it that way, felt like just like in 'Nam: "You do it. You better fucking do it. You better give it to me."

And when they got back, they thought I was a little nutty. My own friends did. They were watching *me*. And I knew that. I felt it. They figured, I guess, I might do it to them what I was doing to him. And I haven't seen them for a while. They went somewhere. I see them once in a while, but on the streets or something. They say "Hi"; I say, "Hi." And they might be saying to someone, "Hey, he *is* fucking loose." Something like that, I don't know. I feel that in the back of my mind when I look at someone. I think that that's what he might have said of me or thinks of me. And that's why I don't see him anymore. Or we don't do the things that we usually do: go up to the Casino and drink or something. Because he might think I'm a little fucking loose, you know. And if I am, I don't know it. I don't *think* I am. I *think* I'm solid up here.

But at times, I lose time somewhere — for about five minutes or something. I think if I don't have somebody with me that knows me, or just the opposite or whatever, that can stop me from doing whatever I'm doing, then I'm all right. And if I don't have somebody with me, I just might hurt somebody badly.

Like my brother O, he used to follow me like a fox. When I'd go to a bar and I'd drink, if I even got into an argument with somebody, he'd be right there. He'd say, "Come on have another one." And I wouldn't be realizing, not until two months or three months. I finally realized, he's with me all the time.

And everytime that I get into something, or talk to somebody, he's right there watching what I'm saying, for some fucking reason. Like he's my baby sitter. And when I finally come out and out with it to him, he told me he was just watching me 'cause I'd hurt somebody.

I said, *"Me?* How do you know that the person that I'm arguing with couldn't hurt me?"

And he said, "Well, I don't know. That's the way it is."

Now, I'm usually on my own.

☆　☆　☆

He came in the house and he went in the bathroom. And when he came out of the bathroom he was talking about "gooks."

And that's when I come in the hallway and I turned around and I said, "Dad, Dad. Come out here." And by the time we got out here, he come at my father and my father tried to grab him and he turned around and he bit my father in the shoulder. It took about five of us to get him down.

And then we took him over to the VA hospital. He was still blacked out. He was still talking about "gooks." And we even told the doctors what he was talking about.

And the doctor turned around and goes, "He looks all right to me."

And we goes, "Well, maybe you think he's all right, but he took a blackout and he tried to kill five people."

And I goes, "That ain't funny, man. There's something wrong with him."

And he turn around and he goes, "He looks normal."

So we just left there and we come home.

He come out of the blackout and he goes, "What are we doing here?"

And we turned around and we told him that he took a blackout.

And he goes, "What do you mean I took a blackout? I was in bed."

We goes, "No you weren't." We goes, "You come out of the bathroom and you tried to kill your father and your cousins."

He told us we were full of shit.

We goes, "We had you over at the VA hospital."

And that's where we had him. We took him back home 'cause they said he was O.K.

My mind snapped for a few minutes. It was weird. While I was hitting her, then I realized what I was doing.

All I remember is I asked her to go outside. Took her outside. Then I just turned around and started slapping her in the face. I really felt bad after that. That wasn't me that hit her, I guarantee you that. 'Cause while I was still hitting her — oh wow! Why would I hit the kid?

We were going to go outside and go for a ride or something. I don't remember why I would ever start hitting the kid. I don't remember nothing. All I remember is her standing there crying — and screaming. Pretty weird. That's when I came back to my senses. I said, "What the hell!" I felt horrible. I didn't know what happened.

I was eight months pregnant and he came home early in the morning. And he went to bed. He had to get up for work, so I went to wake him up. And he wouldn't get up. So I kept on calling him, pushing him to get up. So finally he kicked me in the side. And then he pulled my hair. And then he didn't remember any of it. He said he never did it. After I told him what he did, he said he never did it. And everything that he does, he doesn't remember. So I don't know what it is.

Another time, he come home and he was really out of it. He started yelling at me, and he told me that I loved my mother more than I loved him. He just kept on yelling and everything.

And he said he was going to kill himself. So he went in the bathroom and got a razor and he cut his arms. So he was laying on the floor. There was blood all over the floor. And I didn't know what to do. So I called his mother, and his brother and his sister came over. And he started yelling at them that he hated me. That he was going to kill me.

I didn't know what to do, I didn't know whether I should call the police, because if he wasn't seriously hurt he would probably start on them, or he would start on me for trying to call them. But he started calling me, so I ran down the stairs.

And as I went down the stairs he got up and started coming after me. At the same time his brother and sister were coming up the stairs. So I don't know whether he'd have started on hitting me or not. His sister hid all the silverware so he couldn't get at it again.

And I left him that time again because I was really afraid of what he'd do.

I actually thought I was in Vietnam. I really did. I believed that I was in Vietnam someplace. One of the waiters put his hand on my shoulder. I just turned around and hit him.

And I swore, telling him, "You gook, don't you ever put a hand on me."

Just like you do over the 'Nam.

The Vietnamese people over in Vietnam, most of them are gay. Like the men walking down the street together holding hands. And their way of showing affection and stuff is by rubbing your leg or something like that. So when they come up to you and they did something like that, you just hit them and tell them, "Get away from me."

And when this gook in the Cathay House put his hand on me, I hit him and started throwing tables. I caused a riot in the Cathay House. So they barred me.

The only thing that I know is that when I come in the door, my brother's door was open. So I went to close it, because he sleeps there at night and it was kind of a little chilly. When I turn my back he's in the hallway and he had a knife.

He says, "You ain't going to get me."

And I turn around, "What's the matter?"

And he goes, "You ain't going to get me."

I go, "All right. All right."

And he come at me with the knife. And I turn around and I ran out the door. And then I called my father. And that's when three of us were against him.

And he turned around and he goes, "You ain't going to get me, you motherfucking gooks."

And that's when he turned around and he stabbed me.

My father turned around and got him somehow by the arm. And my brother P had him down too. The next day we told him about it. And when he woke up he didn't know nothing about it.

I went into the joint for a drink. I was working on the docks. I had a hook on my back.

The cop says, "Hey, get your beer and screw."

I said, "What are you talking about?"

Before I knew it, he wacked me. I wacked him back. And I pulled a hook out on him. The thirteen of them, they lugged me out. After he wacked me, I just flipped. I pulled the hook out. And I never knew it.

And I had to go to court for assault and battery with a dangerous weapon. I just remember a lot of blood — my own. They just said I went crazy. I guess I was trying to stab people. I don't know, I just snap off.

They took me over to the hospital and I tried to escape and they got me again. I thought I was back in 'Nam: making a run; trying to get out.

When I woke up I said, "Where am I?" I thought I was on the [medevac] helicopter or something again.

And then when I looked around the doctor says, "Calm down. Take it easy kid." My fucking head was opened up.

I said, "What did I do?" I thought I was fucking captured or something.

Weird things. Me and Q were going down the road. I don't know what happened. I jumped out of the car. I almost killed myself. I wasn't drunk or nothing. He picked me up and threw me back in the car. I was all cut up. I don't know what happened there. I don't know if I opened up the door, I fell out, or what. I guess I jumped out of the car. I don't know. That's what Q told me anyway. I don't know what the fuck happened.

I dream about 'Nam at night sometimes. I wake up sweating and shit. I have a lot of weird dreams and shit. You dream at night. You wake up at three in the morning, I think I'm still over there. That's why I sleep in a separate room upstairs.

You get into a fight, just a regular fight, and you're back in 'Nam. You pull a knife out or something. I get scared I might kill somebody. I don't know. It fucks up your mind. It's weird. I usually sit by myself — things like that. I just don't want to associate with nobody. When I get them weird feelings, I don't want to be bothered with anybody. I just stay away.

I had a few guns and I got rid of them. I was a-scared I might kill somebody. You never know. You might flip out. Sometimes I'd like to just slit somebody's throat. That's the feeling you get: Get him.

Everybody came back from 'Nam almost at the same time. And all of a sudden, just bang! Everybody's: "You ain't gonna beat me." So bang! And these are more or less all friends — or really knows each other. You establish a fucking hate.

It's just a weird feeling: you black out and you really don't know how you're going to act. You try to control yourself and you can't.

And then you might start stabbing a person, and you don't stop or something. And you might even think: Well man, here's a gook or something. Sometimes you just feeling like saying: "Fuck." If you had a rifle or something you'd say, "Fuck everything." Kill everybody.

Somebody says something to you, sometimes you just say, "Forget it." You can let it go. Sometimes you just leap. It's just weird. Sometimes you just feel you're going to go wacky, so you just get away from everybody. You just go by yourself or something. Anywhere.

You walk around. Walk around and "Hi, how're you doing?" You keep going. I might see you out on the street and you say something and I'll cut you, I don't know. You don't know who you're talking to — I don't know.

A lot of people want to start a conversation about Vietnam: how the guys got killed. I don't even like to talk about the shit. I mean, I was in there with a few good friends and a guy in a truck with me got blown in half and he was a real good friend of mine.

And these motherfuckers don't know what they're talking about. And they're yapping off, the fucking assholes. That's what kills me. I got to leave 'cause I'm only going to end up fucking getting into a fight. So you walk away. They don't know what they're talking about. I don't even like to talk about it myself.

You just think: people; you look at them and you say, "Hey man, get away from me," or something. Like I say, it's weird. It's building up in his mind altogether — everything: Vietnam, all this shit. It's all building up on him.

Then one day he gets a rifle and he goes bang: "I never did like these two guys." There's no reason to kill them, but he says: "Well, all right."

Sometimes you feel the pressure. Say you have an argument with somebody. I don't want to argue with the person, I want to get rid of him. If I had a hand grenade, I'd fucking blow him away.

I always fought with my hands. I would never think of picking up a bottle and cracking him over his head and sticking it in his neck. I wouldn't think of that before. Before I went to 'Nam, maybe I might kick you in the nuts or something or in the face. But I mean I wouldn't try to really screw you up.

I even got away from my wife. I had to get away from her. I got one kid, so I had to get out. She was telling my mother I was sick and all this shit. And I went to the doctors and everything.

The guy upstairs gave me some shit — fuck him. [He acts out pulling a trigger.] I just missed him. My wife told me the next day and I said, "Oh, Jesus." I had to go up and talk to the guy.

It happened at my house a few times, and my wife — she left. So I said, "Well, hey, there's no sense in that." She had her father, they come up and he said, "What's wrong?" They all attacked me. Now that's another thing. They all come up, everybody come up. I went fucking wacky. I threw a chair at my father. I said to myself, "Hey man, what is this?" I mean, I was sober and I just went out the back door, jumped over the fence and kept walking. Two hours later I was calm.

They says, "What's wrong?"

I says, "I don't know, leave me alone, that's all. Just leave me alone. Don't bother me and I won't bother you. Just leave me alone. Simple as that."

I don't know, that's the way I feel. I was never like that before.

He's real nervous. He goes crazy. You go up to him and if you grab him, he'll jump away and start putting up his hands. Even talking to him, just talking, he's throwing his hands around. It's hard to explain. He gets into a fight, he goes beserk. He ain't scared of no one or nothing. I think he'd just as soon kill anybody in a fight.

He never says anything. And he doesn't stay in one spot, unless he's playing pool or something. But if he's drinking, he'll have a drink in the club for a while and then leave and then go somewhere else and come back. He just roams around.

Before, when you got in a fight, it was just to win not to hurt. But now I try to avoid fights, because I'd just as soon kill the person than really fight. I never felt that way before. To me, it's not a matter of killing. You ain't scared to kill someone now.

One fight down at the beach when I was home, I used a

beer bottle on a kid. And if he didn't run, I would have probably cut him up real bad.

I try to avoid them. I get shaky. I don't know what goes on. But I just start shaking. I feel like I'm going to lose my mind. That never happened before the service. You just have no control. And you really want to hurt. It's hard to explain.

Before I used to have feelings. I wouldn't really want to hurt no one in a fight. But now it's just a matter of really hurting them. I never had that feeling before. I just don't have no control.

I get scared. Scared I'm going to just lose my mind. I walk away or something to try to calm down. I think if I really got going I'd really hurt someone. I'd grab anything I could near me. I wouldn't be scared to use it. I know a lot of guys that came back don't have control of themselves as far as fighting and respecting people. It's all lost.

Even when I go home, I get in a little argument, I just have to walk away. I get real nervous. I was never like that before. It's a weird feeling.

My wife always says I'd just rather walk away than argue. But I feel it's necessary to just walk away then let it build up. She thinks I just want to drop the subject. See, it seems better to just walk away. It just builds up and I start getting the shakes. Just got to walk away. She wants to sit there and argue it out.

She says I've got to be right all the time. I just avoid the issue of arguing. I just do it so I won't get nervous. But she still says I just walk away and avoid the argument — taking the easy way out.

Where before I went into the service, if I got into a fight I wouldn't think of picking up anything or smashing a skull. But now I wouldn't give it a second thought. There wouldn't be no feelings or nothing. There wouldn't be no emotion. I'd really want to hurt him.

Like up in the Transit when we got in a fight, I didn't remember nothing. I don't know. I just kept on going. I had no idea who I was hitting or anything. It broke up by getting pulled off guys. And the cops came. I guess I lost control.

After the fight, I just didn't remember who I was hitting or anything. They just said I was hitting someone. But I didn't know who. I was just swinging wild. But I didn't remember how I got up or away from the table, or get involved or anything. They just said I was swinging wild at a couple of guys that came in. I don't know who they were.

And I was throwing punches at R. He's a friend. We came in the bar together; we were drinking. We were there for a couple of hours. Then the fight broke out. I wasn't drunk or nothing. It's a weird feeling to be fighting and not know who you were hitting or why. I was shaky, nervous. I was really all jittery. Everybody was talking about the fight. And I didn't know nothing about it.

☆　☆　☆

I get really nervous; like sick. And nothing was helping me. I couldn't sleep at night. I'd be running out of the house and I'd buy a six-pack at two, three in the morning and I'd be riding around. I couldn't even fucking sleep. I really got nervous, you know, all shook up.

And I'd go over to the VA for help.

I'd go up there and I'd tell them, "I want to see a doctor; a psychiatrist; something."

And I was so filled up, you know, and pissed off and everything.

And I used to go up there. And first you'd have like a social worker — which would probably be a Jew — sitting there asking you how it was overseas and, "What did you do?" Giving you the first degree and, "Why do you hate niggers?"

and all this shit. And then he'd be sitting there amazed; staring at you, as if to say, "You've gone through all that? Wow!" Like you're a celebrity or something.

And I'm saying, "I need fucking help, man."

So he'd say, "Okay. I'm going to send you next door to Miss S. And she'll help you."

So I go in there. And there's a fat little spic cunt there.

And she'd be telling me, "Do you smoke [marijuana]? You must smoke," and "You're all doped up," you know, "to be this nervous" and all this shit.

And I'd say, "Fuck no. I need help."

And she'd say something like, "Well, all you Vietnam veterans come in here asking for help. You've just got to learn to help yourself."

And I'm standing there and I'm ready to cry, you know. Either cry or fucking slam her head through the wall.

And I get this face on me I'm trying to hold back and, she's saying, "Now James, are you going to pull a temper tantrum on me, James?"

And I fucking boom! I put a hole in the desk.

And I'd fucking walk down through the corridor and she'd by yelling, "James, come back here, James. James, please come back here, James."

And I'd say, "Fuck you, you cunt."

And then I'd go on the stairs and I'd say, "Nobody cares." Fucking tears would come down me and shit. I felt like fucking bawling you know.

So then I'm like walking around town. And I don't know what to do. I feel like my head's going to spin off me, you know. So like I was standing in the new City Hall Plaza there and I meet an old friend of mine.

He said, "What the matter with you?"

I said "Jeez, I just went up there in the VA to try to get help and they fucked me all around." I said, "My head's going to spin right off me."

And so he says, "Maybe you need a few beers."

So I went over to the Bell and Hand, near City Hall. And after about four beers, I started to relax. And then I felt better, you know. But them fucking assholes.

CHAPTER V

# Democratizing Effects of the War

## 1. *Uniformity and Uniqueness*

THE VIETNAM WAR had a democratizing effect on its partici-
pants insofar as the pattern of flashbacks and violence is
unaffected by race, age, income, education, or geography.
This leveling process was not limited to marines or enlisted
men. Emanuel Bradford is a black who grew up in Louisiana
and then made a career out of the Army. After returning
home from his second tour of duty in Vietnam as a sergeant
first class, he was appointed Noncommissioned Officer-in-
Charge of the Civil Disturbance Committee at Fort Ord. On
November 11, 1972, while holding this title, he fatally shot his
wife in their nearby Seaside, California home.

Although the Vietnam War has had a uniform effect, it was
a unique war for Americans. Both these characteristics
emerge from the narrative of Sergeant Bradford. His experiences in Vietnam were interchangeable with those of the
Boston veterans. In his narrative he recalls that villagers "let
you walk right into the booby traps" and the leader of a Viet
Cong sapper raid turned out to be the base barber. The result
is that "it works on you mentally. Because regardless of
where you are, you know twenty-four hours per day: Will it
happen?" Even that which he is able to "know" is in the form
of a question. In short, "You can't put any trust in anyone."

As further evidence for this view, he describes how he was wounded during an attack on a bunker that he occupied with an American officer. They were there to call in American artillery support for the Arvn. When their Arvn security fell asleep on watch, Viet Cong cut the wire around their position and entered. The Arvn fled.

The only thing that was essentially unique about his experiences in Vietnam was the way they differed from Korea where he had served three tours of duty. The Korean War was in many respects less conventional than earlier wars. But for Sergeant Bradford, "The difference between the Korean War and the Vietnam War is like daylight and darkness." Korea was daylight:

> You had a line of defense in depth all the way back to the rear. You know if a portion of this line is penetrated. And you'll know the exact unit that the penetration was made through. And you'll know whether or not they're coming your way. And you know the best course of action to take. Otherwise, they would make a frontal attack and of course you know if they were making a frontal attack on you.

In Vietnam, Sergeant Bradford found that where there are boundaries to a position they shift suddenly and drastically with the assistance of a technology that has advanced since Korea. Helicopters are his main example of this mobility. Noise is another characteristic of helicopters. The Americans are made more vulnerable and the Viet Cong are made less vulnerable by noise: "When your helicopters come down and put you out in one position, your element of surprise is gone then." Also in Vietnam:

> you only defend strategic points. Like here's a mountain over here to my left and there's a mountain over there to my right. Well, in between the mountain there are spaces that's completely left open. In Vietnam, there's no line to penetrate.

This discussion of battle lines can be treated both literally and figuratively. For what he says about the Vietnamese battle lines also applies to the conceptual lines within the minds of those men who experienced Vietnam and the return home. The demarcations between friend and enemy or time and space are also without a defense in depth; they are also easily penetrated.

A prevalence of enemies, another theme of his experiences in Vietnam, reappeared when he returned home from his second tour of duty there. He had a sense of being continually followed by a car with an unknown driver. He described the elaborate measures he took to "lose contact" with the other driver. This term is borrowed from Vietnam. In the same way it happened vis-à-vis the Viet Cong, no matter what precautions were taken, he always found the pursuer waiting for him.

But, as in Vietnam, the most threatening enemies were not strangers. He was able to explain the unknown driver in terms of his wife: "First thing I thought about was maybe my wife has hired a detective or something to watch *me;* to see what *I'm* doing." This notion also reflects the continual discovery of being outdone by the Viet Cong in matters of reconnaissance. Moreover, the enemy was not undertaking reconnaissance for its own sake. The reconnaissance was a prelude to unknown danger: "Then I said, 'Maybe I'm getting too close to something.' Because my wife don't talk to me, don't cook for me, she doesn't want to do anything at the house."

The process of identifying his wife as an enemy relied on additional assumptions that were borrowed from Vietnam. Most of all, he assumed nothing was as it seemed. If his wife said she was going to the drugstore, he would follow her in his car to confirm it. If he saw her car parked in front of the drugstore, it could be explained by assuming she was unfaithful: "There's a motel and other places behind it." Similarly, he felt it necessary to verify her claim that she was working on the night shift at a hospital. He called her there and spoke to her. But instead of verification, this conversation raised the possibility of a conspiracy against him. When she arrived home, he asked her to explain why she was unwilling to talk at greater length on the telephone:

> "Well, the same time you called, there were a lot of doctors and nurses around." I said, "If you were working, I don't see how you had a chance. What about patients at that time?" I said, "If everyone was standing around, then you should have stayed home. 'Cause I can't see how you were working." I don't know what they did down there. They might have had some party or something lined up. Or maybe were supposed to meet down there, and then take off and go other places.

The "they" he refers to here appeared everywhere. Since nothing was as it seemed, it was not enough to see his wife as the enemy behind the unknown man. He was actively concerned with locating the enemy behind his wife. His closest friends became part of the conspiracy. A recurring possibility for him was that "she could have been blackmailed" by one of them. Alternately, "I felt that someone or some people had completely changed her mind around," and in the process "completely poisoned her mind" against him. The alternatives were the same he described having to contend with in Vietnam where the villagers who were nominally allies were in fact enemies. As he viewed it, the villagers became enemies either through being forced into collaboration by the Viet Cong (who engaged in a form of blackmail by taking sons as hostages) or through being "influenced" by the Viet Cong. Not only was the enemy difficult to determine, but if they were identified their motives were indeterminate.

This quest "just preyed on my mind." An increasing sense of danger developed that at last brought him totally back to

Vietnam. This last stage was reached through a remark that his wife made, or at least which he believes she made. His other accounts of what he had seen or heard around him since returning from Vietnam have not been substantiated. If his accounts of events outside himself are based on misperceptions, they are even more relevant. In any case, there is a pattern to all the descriptions he gives of his emotional responses which indicates accuracy in their case. One evening, eight months and twelve days after returning from Vietnam:

She said, "If you got killed in Vietnam, everything would be okay. I just wish you got killed in Vietnam." That's when the thing happened. It's something it's hard for a person to explain. I have read, I have talked about other people doing things like that. And I said, "It just can't happen. Why would he do a thing like that?" You're just beyond your point of return. It's something that overpowers you and happens to you. You cannot control. It's no stopping. It's no stopping. When she told me that "if you had got killed in Vietnam, everything would be okay," I could just see those bunkers. That's when I was in that French bunker when we got it that night. I could see myself laying there, praying to stay alive, because I had a wife and children at home. And I could just see: I was praying to God, "I can't die. I can't die. I have a wife and children." I even said the twenty-third Psalm. I just said, "The Lord is my shepherd I shall not want. I will fear no evil for Thou art with me." I just kept saying those words over and over and over, when that happened to me.

I don't know, it was just like an enemy to me. Just like an enemy to me. Just something I had to get rid of. It's just something that causes you to reach a point. You're not really dumb to the fact that you're doing something, but it wasn't her. It wasn't her. I'll tell you that. It wasn't her at all that I was actually hurting. It was just an enemy to me. It was just something that had become an enemy. And it was just something that had to be destroyed.

Another indication of the danger that he felt was represented by his wife can be found in the sense of freedom he had shortly after the shooting:

> When I got in jail, it just seemed like I was free. I was just freed from something. I had a terrific burden or a terrific strain on me, but when I got in jail it was just like something lifted up off me. I was just free like a bird, so to speak.

His sense of freedom also reflects the boundaries that were finally imposed on his world by a jail. But the incongruity of these feelings in this setting meant the boundaries soon became as oppressive as their absence had been.

## 2. *The Families*

The democratizing effect of the War can also be seen through the eyes of widely varied families to which veterans returned. These families saw the same sort of alteration that was observed by the Boston families and they responded to it in much the same way.

Byron Eugene Gann was charged with killing his stepfather six months after returning from Vietnam to his home in Cleveland, Tennessee. His mother regarded him as "always even-tempered" before Vietnam. Afrerwards:

> He was real nervous. And he couldn't sleep. He didn't want to go to bed. He just wanted to sit up in a chair and sleep. And when I finally would get him to go to bed he would have nightmares. And he was just real nervous.

Following Vietnam, and before the shooting, he was his own enemy:

> By the time I got home, well, he said he was going to kill himself. And he got in the car and tried to kill himself — tried to turn the car over. He ran into a bank and ruined the two front

wheels. And then he got it back in the yard and climbed up on it and kicked the windshield and broke it.

Throughout this period, Byron (or Barney, as he was called by his family) and his stepfather were real good buddies. Whatever one did the other was in there helping him. When one had money they both did. They both drank and they liked to work on cars together. He helped us paint. Barney went with us twice and helped us finish a paint job that we had started.

However, four days before the shooting "he was telling about things back when he was a child that his daddy did. And I never heard him mention them." Specifically, "He was telling about his daddy killing his calf. He was about five years old."

His sister testified in more detail about the calf that was named Barney. "It was born on his birthday." In Byron's presence, "my father killed it for food" by striking it on the head with a hammer. Their father then ate the calf at dinner and "he tried to force us to."

When her brother returned from Vietnam, she noticed that:

He had changed. Well, he seemed to be concerned about death. He was worried about killing someone, not only the Vietnamese but even American soldiers. There were so many that were buried in mass graves. And he was afraid that the parents or the relatives would not know where they were. And he seemed to be preoccupied with this. He came to visit us for a week. And he was very quiet. He didn't talk about it very much, but I am sure he was preoccupied with it. He was almost listless, I would say. Maybe far away. And I know the friend he went over with. I believe that he, I don't know whether he saw him, but he stepped on a land mine. And when Byron came home, the first thing he told me at the airport was they did not find his friend's head.

There is a sequence to Byron's memories that is logical if time and space are no longer relevant. The head was central to the death of a close friend in Vietnam. The head was also central to the death of a close friend in childhood. The childhood friend was himself insofar as it bore his name. The murderer was his father. His stepfather was now acting as his father. The setting for the murder was a farm, such as the one where "Barney" was killed. But this was not a sequence that Byron could express to either his mother or himself:

He seemed to not even realize that anything had happened. This was from the very beginning from the first time I saw him until about, just a few minutes ago. He seems to have no realization of what has happened.

☆   ☆   ☆

Walter Lee Treadwell, Jr. returned from Vietnam to his middle class home in Whittier, California. His father observed that "he would seem to be under extreme pressure." On the night of February 22, 1972 he fought his father, destroyed part of their home and then held his mother captive at gunpoint until he was shot by the police. Referring to the beginning of this episode, his father recalls, "I don't believe I ever saw him in such a state that he was in that night. It was total belligerence. And not caused by anything that was so profound." The scope of this transformation can be measured by the mother's account:

My own fear was more like just being frozen. And I especially had no sense of time. I had no sense of shaking and crying — that kind of fear. I just could not comprehend reality; that what was really real; that it was really happening. I had no sense of reality whatsoever. I had this frozen, this unreal sensation, about the whole thing.

Then Lee said, "I'm hit." And I said, "I don't believe it." And it was, my saying that, was just some more of the feeling that I had for two hours. That I didn't feel like I could believe any of it. That there was just no sense of reality about anything that was happening. I could never see that Lee was shot. I never did see that he was shot and I don't know if even my mind believed it. I don't believe my mind believed that he was shot at all.

# CHAPTER VI

# A Texan

BORGER, in the Texas panhandle, declared its patriotism through a billboard on the edge of town. The sign included a continually updated total of American casualties in Vietnam.

It was not through his murder trial that Truman Smith first became well know in Borger. He had been a high school football hero. He went on to college, but left to join the Army. During his first assignment, in the Panama jungles, he sent home a photograph of himself wearing a uniform and a smile; it was inscribed: *"What me worry?"*

The initial part of the following narrative is in the form of extracts from letters that Truman wrote to his parents while he was in Vietnam. They present the most positive picture of the War that he could manage. For these letters were intended to reassure both his parents and himself. The casualties inflicted on his battalion are, for the most part, omitted. Nevertheless, the letters are helpful for tracing the stages of his immersion in Vietnam. As an example, the initial reference to homecoming plans included a return to college. Truman, at that point, was still able to see civilian life for its own sake; the boundary around it was intact. The homecoming was soon defined as no more than a contrast to Vietnam. Thereafter, it was not referred to in any form.

Although Truman usually wrote home in an offhanded way about his attempted adjustment to warfare, this was also part of his attempted self-reassurance. For his letters contain no overt reference to the second front that he later recalled encountering in Vietnam: "I was an animal. I fought very hard to become one, and then when I became one I fought hard to not be one. I fought a war in my mind." But this internal warfare is implied throughout his correspondence. A letter describing what he considers the most callous act of his fellow soldiers is followed by his most poetic letter: a description of the Vietnamese landscape.

In spite of their intent, these letters reflect his inability to take anything at face value — starting with his discovery that hot weather means Christmastime and "friendly" villages mean ambushes. Along the way, he is also forced to see past his articles of faith. As one was contradicted by the realities of combat, another emerged that frequently reflected an official Army decree. Essentially, the process was one of discovering that what had been a certainty was in fact an article of faith. The variety of contradictions between one letter and another, and sometimes between one sentence and another, had a cumulative effect. They made it difficult to order the world. This difficulty was particularly great because the articles of faith were often a reason for being in Vietnam. The resulting disorder is reflected in the overlapping, and eventually the merger, of increasingly dissimilar categories. Sacred and profane are no longer distinguished by the end of these excerpts. Initially, the tombs of a cemetery are bypassed; later they are trampled. The distance between life and death disappeared. This convergence first applied to others, but before long he applied it to himself. Less than two months after arriving in Vietnam, he cannot decide whether he prefers to live or die. If he is momentarily incapable of self-reassurance at this point, he is permanently incapable of it by the end of these letters.

☆ ☆ ☆

*17 December*

Dearest Parents,

Can you believe it? I have finally made it to Vietnam. Maybe I can see some real combat for a change. For the last two years, I, along with most of the men in the company, have had nothing but simulated warfare. Training continuously for war and never getting to see it is some letdown. It is really a true honor to be able to prove yourself worthy of Americanism.

☆ ☆ ☆

*30 December*

Cu Chi has been our base camp for the last two weeks. I guess what we are doing is just getting the unit adapted to the elements of war and conditions of weather. Right now it is pretty hot and humid, but the monsoon season is not far off. Then, I hear, it gets fairly cool.

Christmas was not too bad on most of the guys, because with the weather like it was, it just didn't seem like Christmas and was easy to put out of the mind.

☆ ☆ ☆

*16 January*

Today I am sitting in a rice field, we have a village surrounded. This village was supposed to be friendly, but so far we have had several sniper shots from there.

*18 January*

We just moved into a small perimeter about 400 meters from our last base camp. Our plan is this: We're going to meet up with Companies "A," "B," and "E" around midnight and run a raid on a VC camp. I hope they don't have any idea we're coming, but most likely they do. They're in a village pretending to be civilians, and we're to destroy the whole village. If the people we kill aren't VC, then they are aiding the VC, so it makes them just as guilty as being one. I know I'm not supposed to tell this or write it, but by the time you or anyone reads this, we'll have already done it.

On the way up to this place we're at right now, I've been having a lot of trouble from my men. One of my men refused to carry the other part of the demmo, and he was one of the few men who wasn't carrying something extra. I've had trouble with this man before, but at that time, I overlooked his behavior; this time, no. He is Negro and thinks he is always being picked on because of that fact. That isn't so. I'll tell you one damn thing, I ordered him to carry it til every ounce is blasted. Of course, I'm going to fire mine first.

I didn't have time yesterday to write anything. The raid didn't come off at all. What happened is that we all moved out, like I was telling you, from a rubber plantation in trucks. We lucked out this time and didn't have to walk. Where we were going was quite some distance from there. We hadn't gone but maybe three miles, and came up to a bridge that the Cong had just knocked out, so we were making it on foot. We didn't have the time to get to the village before morning.

*21 January*

They say tomorrow about 0500 hrs., we start out for about two months. God, that's a long time to stay on the move, but I can take it. This unit is Airborne and can — and I'm Airborne; therefore, I must be able to take it.

After this two months we may move all the way to the DMZ, but it's still not for sure. I've got the feeling it's true. You know, it's hell here, but I think if I go a little over, and extend for two months, when I get out it'll be December. That will be just in time to go the last semester of college and have a little extra cash. I don't know if I'm going to do it, or not, just yet. It might not be such a good idea.

*23 January*

Today is Tuesday and guess what happened. We started out yesterday and even got to the place we were heading. We rode in a Copter for forty-five minutes and went seventy-two miles northeast, landed, started to march out to our objective, then got the word that we've got to come back. That was some letdown after preparing for it for so long.

Well, we came back, and now for the real blow. We're going to Da Nang, or it's close, Phu Bai. It's an Air Base, and we're going to surround it and provide protection for the next thirty days.

*23 January*

There's a small P.X. that isn't but about one or two hundred meters from where I sit, and some of the guys have gone over and bought some drinks. One of the guys brought me one, and all they had left was unsweetened grapefruit drink. Terrible shit. The people here keep ordering it, because they think the American GI likes it, but the GI buys it only because he can't get anything else. They run out of Coke, so they know you'll buy the stuff; and the GI will, I know — I'm one. The stuff costs about twice as much as in the States.

*25 January*

Well, we finally got to Phu Bai. The marines don't like us being here. One reason is, this has been their area ever since the war started. Man, they have really been getting it, but good! I think that's one reason we're here. I thought we were to protect an air base at Phu Bai, but now I know it was only for security reasons. We are here to fight, and it looks like we're in it deep. Right now we're thirty-four miles from the DMZ, and the Cong pretty well runs this area. They move freely, with hardly anyone to stop them.

We moved out yesterday from Phu Bai. We are now dug in at a cemetary "grave yard" and this place is as big as Borger and Buenavista combined. Say about eight by ten miles.

It's about 0700 hrs., and we are to move out to some place for a little search and destroy mission. We should be back to this cemetary by sometime tonight. That is, if we don't get it too bad out there.

The marines got it bad the other day, somewhere around four-hundred dead — but that happens to them every-other-day or so. I can see why. "Mr. Charley VC" is something else in this area.

*26 January*

Yesterday on the search and destroy mission, we had the 1st Cavalry fighting with us. That is, all units are working together now. Not like in the States where all units are in competition with each other, but more like Americans doing a job that needs to be done in a family manner. It seems like the

Marines let the Cong just plain over-run the place, and we are here to cut down on so much aggression.

We cleared out about five to seven miles of territory and found no VC, but the 1st Cavalry had a few casualties from booby traps. We stayed there until today, then moved on back to this damn cemetery. Damn! The reason I say "Damn" cemetery is because we have to be careful not to disturb any graves. The big chief of the nearby village doesn't like his elders stepped on, shit on, or slept on, — so that's the way the cookie crumbles.

The reason we were so filthy — we went through some woods that some napalm was dropped on, and everything was charcoal.

You know, now is a good time to have a camera. You should see the mountains and valleys. It's really beautiful here.

I think I've told you about tripping the booby trap, but I'm not for sure. There's not much to really say about it. Almost everyone who comes here sets off at least one. The only thing is, a big percentage of the booby traps here that the Cong set, don't work; but you are never sure when one will, because some definitely do. The booby traps I'm talking about are made mostly of explosives. Punji pits aren't of too much concern, because few are in as much wide use as explosives. At the beginning of the war, Viet Cong didn't have enough explosives, but now they have plenty. Punji sticks are made of bamboo sharpened on one end with human waste baked into it. If stuck, it's just enough to remove someone to a hospital for a week or so. Usually the wound is in the foot or leg area. The only thing is, it gets one man out of the field with a bad infection. With an explosive, it's possible to take not only the one who sets it off, but also two or three more men.

*29 January*

We're moving out on an ambush mission tonight, not far from here, to try to catch a few Cong that have been throwing a little too much mortar fire at our base camp. Yesterday they blew hell out of a tank about 100 meters from the front of our perimeter. Killed one, and ripped hell out of the other men in the tank crew. They were all medivaced away to a hospital within ten minutes.

*30 January*

We didn't get any VC last night, but the 1st Cavalry got into it on the other side, most of the night. We're back in base camp now, a little north of Phu Bai.

And now comes the bad word: We leave in the next hour for the D.M.Z.

The 1st Cavalry got it bad last night. They lost a lot of men. We're going to get some of those three divisions of N.V.A. before the week is out. Well, all I've got to say is, I'm ready to go, and I know I can take it because I'm Airborne. Ha!

*2 February*

I've worn the same clothes for the last two weeks. We have only one pair now, so we just wash this one pair when we can. If this pair gets torn up badly enough, we get resupplied. I'm not complaining, because our officers haven't got to change either, and they smell just as bad as we do. Yes, we don't need to be shot, we already smell dead.

*3 February*

We have cleared the village and are now starting to go south to block the VC. We just received fire and some of our men have been hit. The VC took up a bunker line to our front. Between us and the Cong is a rice field about fifty meters across. Behing the Cong is "B" Company, and "D" Company is pushing to our left front. Rifle fire and shrapnel are flying all around! God Amity! Is there a good place to hide? They've got us penned down, and we've got them penned down!

☆ ☆ ☆

*5 February*

We have been fighting hard for two days, and it looks bad for us. We have lost some ten or fifteen out of our company.

One of the South Vietnamese soldiers gave me some candy. First he invited me into his home, a really nice house, that the 105's just completely tore apart. Then his family came into the rubble that was once their home, and when I saw the tears and heartbreak, that almost did it. I don't like this war, and yet, I can see for myself it's necessary. We've got to win! So these people can return to their homes and be certain it will be a free home, and not be riddled by gunfire or shattered with bombs.

I got a 45 off a M-79 Gunner, stuck it to one of the people that was a prisoner, and had the interpreter tell him if he didn't stop giving so much trouble, I was going to blow his guts out. He kept on squirming around trying to get away and co-operating none at all, so I blew him away. The other prisoner we had co-operated very quickly.

This place is really a wreck. Man, it was a nice place, too. It was about the size of Phillips, Borger, and Buenavista put together, say about fifteen miles square. Now it's levelled to the ground. We're going to be here all night. We just got through pushing all the civilians out of the town to a close-by secure area. There, we can keep an eye on them, and at the same time, have them out of the way in case we get into it again. They also can't be trusted, it is a little hard to tell them apart, VC or civilian.

We recovered some of the dead we had to leave behind the other day. The Cong poked their eyes out and cut their bodies up to where most had their intestines dangeling out and drug on the ground as our men carried them. Thank God they were dead. If they hadn't been dead, we wouldn't have left them behind.

I hope the Cong give us trouble tonight — we're ready this time.

*6 February*

We had no trouble last night.

People wonder why a guy comes back from a place like Vietnam and acts like an animal. Well, I myself have changed just in the last three days. I'm hard on the inside, and as far as I'm concerned, if anyone stands between me and my job, I'd just as soon kill 'em. Life isn't worth much anyway, besides, some of those people are better off dead.

It's been cool for so long, I don't think I'll ever see the sun again. It's wet, too, and about forty degrees all the time. This is the Central Highland, and I'm cold, dirty, and tired. Sometimes I just don't know whether I give a damn if I die or not. A lot of guys here feel the same as I do.

The feeling you get when walking through rice paddy after rice paddy, never getting that well-earned rest, is the wish for a sniper to shoot at you, or for a little action of any sort.

*9 February*

We have been constantly on the move, trying hard to get the rest of the Cong that we ran into the third of February. On the fourth we had four men killed and eleven wounded. That's not really bad, considering that the battle we had was one of the longest and largest scale of the war here in Vietnam, and it hasn't ended. Charley Company led most of the attack, we had been moving all over this area, trying to find the rest of the Viet Cong.

There are supposed to be three phases of their last stand here, something like Custer's last stand. This is it for them if they can't divert us, then I guess that's it, and we come home winners again. They are sort of in their last stage of the three phases of their last stand. The VC's first phase was to try and make the American Forces disperse; they've already tried that and failed. Their second phase was to try and take some or most of the large compounds, cities, and base camps; they did this a little, but were overcome in the long run. Their third phase, which they are in now, is massive attacks and stand offs which aren't looking good for their side.

*10 February*

Oh man, last night was rough! We had a small engagement. The Cong tried to come into our perimeter that the company had set up here in a village south of the town. They had about three R.P.G. [Rocket Propelled Grenades]. They fired the dickens out of us.

*13 February*

We are now called the "Hobo Battalion," because we have no more than what we carry on our backs. I hope that's not a permanent name. I know we're some of the toughest ones here in Vietnam. We don't even carry ponchos or air mattresses anymore. It's still 13 February. We just had our C.O. killed.

*14 February*

For some time now, all the teams in the platoon have been taking turns for listening post. I asked the Platoon Leader to alternate. My men are exhausted and are beginning to do a sloppy job. They have just about had it, and that goes for me too.

*1600 hours*

We saw Charley first. We pulled back about 200 meters from him and artillery is now pounding hell out of his position. We have one guy wounded. Looks like today we carry the ball. We caught up with Mr. VC about an hour ago. I guess we'll be here for a while clearing the area. Right now we are sitting back until the artillery and air strikes are over.

Well, about the food and stuff that is offered to the GI over here. I know every once in a while some civilians try to sell you a coke with chipped glass or with battery acid in it, but to tell you the truth, most of the people make so much money off the GI that they won't let anything like that happen. They want your money more than they want your life.

☆   ☆   ☆

*15 February*

The fight we started about 1700 hr. on the 14th just after the artillery stopped, we went in the village. Just as we got to the edge of the village, I was taking my team to the left rear flank and one of my men got a hand grenade thrown at him. He wasn't fast enough and got both of his legs blown off. I turned just in time to see him come falling out of the air.

About ten minutes later I had all my fire team to the left flank. I jumped a small hedgerow and ran to a house I thought the grenade came from. I threw a grenade through a hole in the wall, and just at that moment, I saw that there were three Cong in the rear of the house. I was holding my M-16 in my left hand and was trying to get clear of the house, and was shooting at the Cong at the same time. They threw two grenades at me. One went off at the same time the one I threw in the house went off as I was going down for cover. I caught a piece of schrapnel in the left leg and the concussion rolled me across the ground. I think I shot one Cong, maybe two. I don't know, and I don't care.

Today I feel ok, so I didn't think it necessary to be taken out of the field. I don't want the guys to think I'm sissy, although to tell you the truth, anyone would like to get out of the field. We are going on toward Quang-Tri, clearing all the way.

It's about noon now, and we should make contact again today. Yesterday we levelled one section of the village, burning everything in our path, and it didn't bother me at all. I was shook up about my man getting the shit knocked out of him, and me getting the hell knocked out of me.

I shouldn't tell you this, but the other day a man was playing around with a hand grenade. You can unscrew the top of a hand grenade, break the blasting cap off, and screw the top back on. The grenade is then useless; except for pulling the pin and chasing the little kids away by throwing the grenade at them. The kids will continuously bug hell out of you for food if you let them — and most of them have more than we do.

Anyway, the man I mentioned did this to his buddy, by

handing it to him. While they were arguing, the hand grenade went off. Killed both of them. Heads, arms and legs were everywhere. He must have thought it was harmless! He got the wrong grenade.

*24 February*

Every time we kill a Cong, we cut his left ear off. I tried it once, but after I did, I couldn't stomach it. That is, doing it to someone dead — alive, Ok, dead, No! I didn't think I would have the stomach to watch or let someone else do it, but I have acquired a stomach for that much. Some of the men get their kicks by safety-pinning their combat patch to the forehead of the ones they kill. Boy, does war change a man's ideals!

You have to fight mostly against losing your mind, along the same principal as losing your life, so I can understand what my men are doing.

☆  ☆  ☆

*27 February*

Looking back toward LZ Jane that sits in the mountain's edge, was like looking at a very beautiful picture; painted blue-black mountain background with deep blue streaked with crimson sky. And there was a line of broken pure white clouds almost in the center, just above LZ Jane. From LZ Jane there came a chalk and light brown dirty road that crossed level green rice paddies.

☆  ☆  ☆

*7 March*

Sp/4 T in our platoon got pissed off at our Platoon Sergeant U, and T, being a M-79-man, shot a grenade at his bunker. It blew hell out of the bunker, but didn't hurt anyone. The 1st Sergeant heard it and came storming down the hill.

He grabbed poor T and beat crap out of him, then dragged him up to the Command Post. Nothing happened, though, because T claimed it was an accident. In a combat zone a person can just about do anything and get away with it.

When I get home (if ever), I have a good idea of what I'll do for the first month. I'll stay home, watch T.V., sleep a lot, and never drink Kool-Aid again. I've had enough of it, but still, it tastes better than the warm piss they call water here. I'll buy a hamberger and pizza almost every day, and I'll exercise very little, so I can gain some weight back.

*10 March*

Later on the same day, we came across 3 dead VC who had been dead about a week and a half. Maggots were crawling out of their eyes and mouth. The water they were laying in was really yellow, and the stench in the air was thick enough to chew — as if anyone would want to. We are all fairly used to these scenes by now, but you should have seen the new men in the company get sick. That made me feel like an old soldier for a change; I guess really I am.

*11 March*

You asked in your letter about this "stopping the bombing over North Vietnam." We have got to kill the NVA and slow down the VC before there is peace in Vietnam. We must clear the Cong out completely; that is the only way. Bombing in the North helps us little guys get the job done, and we are doing a damn good job.

*12 March*
Last night while on ambush patrol, in separate platoon missions, the 3rd Platoon caught something like 150 VC's. That's more than a company. They really screwed up and let the VC go right through. They thought there were too many to try and take, which in my opinion was a bad decision, because we have more fire power in one platoon than in any battalion of NVA.

*14 March*
As we were setting up in what looked like a hell of a good place for the Cong to use an avenue-of-approach, we set out trip flares in places that we couldn't watch closely. About five minutes later, one of our men set one off accidentally, because some idiot set one up behind him as he was setting his up. He claims that he didn't know there was one already being set up there. It lit up, and just about gave our position away. We saw nothing, though; we must have either done a good job yesterday and last night, or just plain goofed up a good ambush.

You know, it's been weeks since I've shot a duck or a chicken, or burned down a house or two; so today as we went back through the place, I got my chance. I just shot and burned everything in sight.

*17 March*
Last night we went on an ambush at the edge of AP Nho Lam and took twenty Arvn troops with us. These guys are really sorry. They take everything with them — chickens, ducks, and pans to cook in. It looks like they would be more careful with their noise. Luckily enough, though, we didn't

see anything, because if we had, we couldn't have expected much from the Arvn.

You know, I'd really like to have a mirror — unbreakable. I haven't seen my face for weeks, and I'd like to see what I look like now.

*18 March*

It was suspected that a man in the sergeant's own squad shot him, but to tell the truth, no one here has any use for him. He spent nearly fifteen years in the Army, behind a desk. It was also a relief for me to see him go; he just wasn't a field trooper. He had been a garrison trooper, and I know for a fact that one of our men shot him to get him out of the field. Most everyone knows it, but they also know that he wasn't worth a damn.

*20 March*

We've lost so many men the past month or so. I guess I've just been trying to keep it back from you — and from myself, too. It's hard to believe that out of 167 men in the company, only 20 or 30 of the original men are left.

I'm not kidding, I want out of this area. I'm scared to death. This place, AP Tan Xuan Lai, is really bad with booby traps and VC; and they have been watching and waiting for us for too long. And it's getting to where the VC are finding out where we are and where we are going.

*22 March*

We started back to To-Thon-Luong Co and moved up to a school house. That night I took just my squad on an ambush about 1000 meters from the school house to a graveyard which was west of there. This time we weren't caring too much whether we were stepping on graves or not.

Then we came back to AP Pho Nam where one of my men got hit by a 105 round that was one of our own.

Truman's father died soon after the last of the excerpted letters. When he returned home for the funeral, his first words, according to his sister-in-law, were "Where's the stiff?" He only recalls that "I felt like he had taken my place in death." Just as Vietnam defined his father's death, the funeral defined his return there: "I went [back] to Vietnam for one particular reason — that was to die." With no boundaries to intrude, each death merged with the other. While others went through the brush, he walked along an exposed trail that led him, knowingly, into an ambush. He was severely wounded by a Viet Cong that he had earlier left for dead. While lying on the trail, Truman also left himself for dead and saw it accomplishing a further objective: "I thought I was dead. It was a big relief. Now I was one of my buddies."

Truman Smith seen as a veteran by his friends:

[Before Vietnam he was] always a friendly, warm, outgoing person. [Afterwards he was] very withdrawn and within himself.

I said "Hey," and he practically tore the stove out in trying to get behind it or something. [He later said] "Damned, I thought you were a Cong."

He'd come home from school and he'd sit there and he'd say: "I'm not really here."

He whirled around and said, "Don't ever stand behind me."

[While at a gas station] trains collided with each other — they made a real loud bang. He hit the ground and he took off running across the street. It was no split second thing. The whole thing took a minute to a minute and a half. What got me, he came back and he didn't seem nervous or anything. He just gave me the money and left.

A tremendous hardness came over him. He looked at me like I was a feared enemy.

Truman Smith seen as a veteran by himself:

I had a deadly fear of myself. I had a fear of killing somebody. That somebody would pat me or touch me on the back. I went to a psychiatrist and he said I had to do it myself. He said it was a natural reaction.

I didn't have any memories of before I went into the army. All I had were memories of killing people.

[In a dream Borger actually was in Vietnam.] Our Borger base camp is being invaded. And here we are drawn out to the perimeter to fight the gooks. And just outside the perimeter they had gathered into the kitchen cabinets and stairwells.

I knew I was in Vietnam. A bee stung me on the back and I dropped the log and crawled 20 feet or 20 yards and I jerked off my shirt, because I was sure I was hit. I said, "God, I've been hit." And I looked up and I saw my brother and I said, "What are you doing here?"

It's [the death of a friend in Vietnam] just like it happened days ago. Or maybe minutes ago.

Everyone's so careless here, you never know who's on your side or whose side you're on.

There are several reasons for the continual merger of Vietnam and Borger in the following references by Truman to the

murder that he committed almost two years after returning
home. Since the account was provided on the eve of his trial,
Truman was under the extreme stress that facilitates flashbacks. Further, he was discussing a time of extreme stress —
not only the murder itself, but the events immediately preceding it. The victim, Allen Greer, drove Truman to a local
airport one night after they had been drinking together. The
reason for the trip was unclear to Truman. Since he had been
living with Allen's wife, Truman considered himself in danger.

In addition, the site of the murder, even from an objective
point of view, was similar to Vietnam in various ways. For
instance, alongside the road leading up to it there was an
abandoned truck that had been destroyed by fire: "I remember the flashback of a burned-out tank. It looked exactly like
a bombed-out tank."

Because the shooting itself was a situation where Truman
felt he was in Vietnam, it is not surprising that he would relate
to it, and relate it, through flashbacks. During a visit to the
murder site, Truman was retracing his steps up the hill to the
landing field when he suddenly said, referring to Allen, "He
was walking to my point." (The lead man in a military patrol
is referred to as the "point.") The airfield, or landing zone, in
Vietnam is usually a kind of sanctuary. Accordingly, when
Truman noticed he was about to step on the runway, he inter-
rupted his own commentary on an unrelated subject to ver-
balize a flashback: "I felt easy when I was right here with
him." Shortly afterwards, when Allen hit him on the head
with a flashlight, Truman killed him with seven shots from a
pistol.

The extent to which time, as well as space, was out of joint
could be seen at the police station later that night when he
gave his weight as 195 pounds. Upon hearing about it later,
he expressed surprise, since "That's what I weighed before I

went into the service." There was another linkage across time; his father died on May 8, 1968; the murder occurred on May 5, 1970.

The disjointed way in which his comments are presented here reflect the disjointed way in which they were originally presented.

I really liked the guy. I despised him a little bit. One minute he's friendly, the next minute you catch him saying something about your friend. I was afraid he'd shake my hand and stab me in the back with the other.

He said he had some friends over there in niggertown that he could get some liquor off of. It's a separate village. Borger is an LZ [Landing Zone.] It's my territory. The Cong are over there. Bien Hai is safe. I don't trust black people. Allen had more friends over there than I did.

I still felt we had a long way to go to get back to our company area — I mean to get back to town — to the phone [after misplacing the car keys].

I didn't know he hit me. I felt pain in my head.

I remember having fears more than anything. If you've been physically hurt, you almost give up your life rather than have to be in a hospital bed for eight months. It's the lying there — the suffering.

I had shot him [a Viet Cong] approximately four times. His guts were hanging out. I didn't have the time to kick the rifle from his hand. Like a fool, I just kept on going [and was shot seven times by the same Viet Cong].

It was instinct: "Possibly this is going to happen again." I was taking a precaution.

I've worked a lot of training out of my mind. I react by instinct.

My hand was there. I didn't know the gun was there. There was just flame coming out of my hand. That was the same place that 150 gooks came through.

I can see him just like I see Congs die. I can see him fall and twist and turning a dark color. And I can even see him with a sort of a uniform on; he had a black shirt on.

After I done it there was nothing in my mind. I went completely blank. I didn't know who he was. Then I realized: "It's Allen Greer. He's dead, man."

I believe I can hear his name echoing back from the mountains, 'cause I was screaming — but my mouth wasn't moving.

[He then undressed the body.] In Vietnam you strip the [Viet Cong] body so it won't be booby-trapped. I've had buddies killed by dead Viet Cong.

I told my brother it was the first real person I ever killed. Vietnam is not the world. The United States is the world.

# CHAPTER VII

# A New Yorker

ANDREW PIESZALA joined the Army after dropping out of high school in New York City. Looking back on it from Attica Prison, he wrote:

> I was gung-ho about fighting to keep communism out of my country. But like most of us green necks, after thirty days in 'Nam you found out what the real meaning was. And although you didn't want no part of it, it was too late to turn back now.

His disenchantment during the War and since has evolved to a point where the United States, not communism, is the enemy:

> You have more of a chance to survive in war than you have in a society such as ours, where promises and lies make up the majority of the supporting structures of a democrat society.

The following narrative is comprised of interviews with Andrew while he was jailed in Buffalo, before his transfer to Attica. He was convicted of murdering Michelle and William Deyl in Cheektowaga, New York. The scar on his neck resulted from one of several suicide attempts. Since returning from Vietnam, he has alternated between evening scores against others and himself.

By his account, it was in Vietnam that he first found the

means of evening scores — usually against other Americans.
His description of life after Vietnam is dominated by his
efforts as a combatant at evening scores and his efforts as a
civilian at preventing these scores from being evened. (One
of these acts as a civilian consisted of changing his name from
Charles Ventura — the name he had in Vietnam.)

The conflict between his selves focused on Michelle Deyl.
He describes his "love" for her. He also believes it necessary
to even a score with her. Her rejection of him by mail in
Vietnam became entangled in his mind with an injury inflicted
on him by the Viet Cong. His rage goes far beyond her, but
she is the most accessible part of a "democrat society" and the
war he helped it wage. After acquiring a gun to kill her, he
sent her letters about how she was endangered by it. His
efforts at thwarting himself moved beyond letters. On one
occasion he arranged his arrest by choosing a public place to
point his pistol at a woman whom he claims to have thought
was Michelle.

As he describes it, the murders resulted from an attempt at
avoiding them. He was after the ransom money that would
allow him to travel far enough to be safe from his violent im-
pulses. But this plan did not allow for the extent to which the
combatant would take over from the civilian. Perhaps fore-
seeing this possibility, he drove to the Deyl home at 90 miles
an hour on bald tires.

Thoughts of self-destruction again emerged after the
murders. He recalls thinking that he should arrange to be
killed by a policeman, but he was afraid that only a wound
might result: "What if I just fucking hit me in the leg or in the
stomach or something?" This inadvertent use of "I" shows
how he and the policeman are indistinguishable at this point.
They both want to apprehend him. Andrew had found he was
unable to apprehend himself in any sense. He could no more
arrest himself than he could understand himself. He wanted to

die "fast," in contrast to the prolonged deaths he saw in Vietnam. Just as during combat "when the guy screams I can feel that scream emerging in my own throat," he shot William Deyl a second time because "I didn't want to see him suffer."

The pressures of both his present confinement and Vietnam are superimposed on each other. This is reflected in the way his descriptions of Vietnam and civilian life are superimposed on each other. In short, he was not able to describe his combat experiences with the detachment of veterans in somewhat less harried circumstances. As a result, it is probable that the accuracy of his Vietnam recollections was affected — as measured by an objective reality. At the same time, his account of the shooting, as well as its prelude and aftermath, contain elements that are imaginary. The camouflaged "coveralls" he recalls wearing before the shooting and the "riverbeds" he later escaped through did not actually exist in Cheektowaga. Instead, they belong to the objective reality of Vietnam. Whatever distortions appear in this narrative reflect his subjective reality, for they provide an accurate picture (or film) of his state of mind.

His narrative demonstrates some of the reasons that movies are an appropriate medium for providing veterans with the term flashback. Insofar as he is still a combatant, the term is an accurate reflection of the way Andrew, and movies, are not bound by time and space. Specifically, he is viewing the Deyls as they are transported back to Vietnam. Insofar as he is a civilian, the characteristics of movies allow him to resist the murder of the Deyls by prolonging their life — within his mind. If he can make their deaths part of a scenario, they will be fictitious. Although he does see the Deyls dying, their deaths are deferred through appearing in slow motion. Once the deaths occur, there is a rebirth through seeing the episodes over and over in what he calls a "rerun." Even within the single rerun there are reruns. For Michelle is shown several times on the screen of his narrative as she enters the murder scene.

This is how I came from a cook to a medic. These two VC went between a company of fucking Arvn and a company of our men. And both companies opened up on both sides and wound up wiping out everybody just about. The gooks had a lot of casualties. They had about six men that weren't fucked up. The Americans had fucking fourteen dead. And we lost a lot of medics. So they came around asking guys if they want to be a field medic. 'Cause all there was to a field medic was to stop the bleeding, and use your best judgment in calling in a helicopter.

So I said, "Yeah. Fuck it, let me get out of here." So I went out in the field.

And around March I had gotten a letter from Michelle. She was only writing me about once every eight days or so. And I knew when a letter would come. I got like this sixth sense. I know when a letter gets there. And so I'd be right there in the line. No shit, I'd be there. And I used to think, maybe I'm a magician or something.

But anyway, I had gotten this letter and I forgot what she said, but she was fucking up somehow. So I got pissed off. And I was dazed and everything. I was out in the field and a fucking mortar barrage started. One of the mortars hit a fucking tree. The fucking top part came down and fucked up my leg. I got a piece of shrapnel over here. There's supposed to be still a piece here. They didn't want to fuck with that. So anyway, I was all fucked up then. I was pissed off.

I wrote back and told her, "You fucking bitch. You fucked me up." I was really pissed off. They put on a fucking cast.

The company next to us had this sergeant in charge of supplies. I used to trade him a whole bottle of Darvons, we

used to get it by the fucking case, for a case of steaks. And
this second lieutenant, just came in the company, was fucking
him. He threatened to throw him in Long Binh jail. They
beat the fuck out of you in there. Steaks and all this meat that
we were getting from him was supposed to be distributed out
anyway. It's perishable. So within thirty days they have to get
rid of it all somehow.

And the Army don't like to throw away food. So they wind
up giving it to some dogface out in the field. So these guys
wouldn't like it. If it isn't good enough for me to eat, they
want to send it out to some guy out in the field. Fuck that.

This lieutenant wanted them steaks to give somebody to
butter up his promotion. He found out about it, so he was
going to give him a court martial for stealing government prop-
erty. So that's where he fucked up, when he started fucking
threatening. That afternoon they placed a grenade under the
front wheel of the jeep in front of the CO's room.

And one guy ran out and threw a fucking grenade; fragging
the fucking office. They got the fucking CO. He was only a
first lieutenant. The second lieutenant comes flying out the
door and jumped in the jeep. He put it in clutch. The concussion ripped the whole top of his body off. It just landed in
the back seat.

So they shake down this company. They shook down this
company. And they found fucking M1 rifles — there wasn't
supposed to be any fucking M1 rifles except in the Arvn
camps. And they found fucking AK-47's. They found fucking rockets. They found everything in this camp. But they
didn't find no fragmentation grenades. And they were pissed
off as hell, 'cause they had all kinds of fucking shit in there,
but they had no frags. This guy told me they had a fucking
four cases. He says they buried them so they couldn't bring no
charges against anybody.

Then there was a time we had a lieutenant colonel. We

called him a "major." Nobody even respected him as a major,
let alone as a lieutenant colonel. But anyway he came in, in
place of this other major. And this major fucked with me all
the time. Every time he sees me, he fucking put me on filling
sandbags, or digging fucking bunkers or some bullshit. I got
tired of that shit, so one day I went up to him.

I said, "Sir, why do you keep putting me on fucking bunker
detail and everything. Don't I got a right to have a break
when I get out of the field?"

He says, "If you weren't a fuck-up, I wouldn't have you
digging bunkers and filling sandbags."

I said something under my breath. He asked me what I
said. I said it to myself because I know the fucking guy would
do something worse.

I said under my breath, I told him, "One of these days I'll
get you."

He said, "What did you say?"

I said, "Nothing sir."

He used to fuck with me all the time. So this one time out
in the field, I was in this fucking rocket crater. We got bar-
raged — fucking rockets. Glad they couldn't aim those fucking things. Anyway, I crawled out of the fucking hole. I
didn't see it, but I had gotten hit. I didn't feel it, but my hand
was numb. I pulled the pin on a grenade, and I went to throw
it and my fingers weren't working. It fell out of my hand into
the crater I had just left.

And when I turned around there was this fucking gook in
there with his AK-47. I said, "Damn, somebody must be
looking out after me." That would teach him to sneak up on
me.

So I got back in there. And I opened up the AK-47, a whole
fucking clip, at this motherfucker — the lieutenant colonel.
And I hit three of the fucking gooks and I missed him.

And this fucking lieutenant seen me.

So after the fire fight, he goes to me, "I want to see you." And I hate this motherfucker.

I said, "What do you want to see me for?"

He said, "Don't you know how to say 'sir'?"

I said, "I only say that to my father. Are you my father?" The motherfucker was younger than me. I used to fuck him all the time.

He said, "Don't get smart with me. I'll have you brought up for insubordination."

I said, "You got to get out of the field first."

He knew what I meant. See the guys in the company were all close knit. If one guy was being fucked with, like they tried to place him under guard; they'd get rid of the witness. So he knew it and he didn't want to say anything until we got out of the field.

The lieutenant colonel was saying, "Who was that that killed those three guys?"

The lieutenant said, "He did. He was trying to kill you. He wasn't trying to kill them."

He says, "What are you talking about, lieutenant. The man saved my life. I'm putting him in for a medal."

I'm saying to myself, "Fuck his medal."

So the lieutenant says, "Yes, sir."

He turn around and look at me, "I'll get you one of these days, Ventura."

I just stuck my tongue at him. We used to do that to them all — disrespect and everything. I used to get away with shit. They wouldn't dare say anything, because they knew if they got fucked up and needed my attention I might wait for the motherfuckers to bleed to death before I got to them. I could always fall back on the excuse, "Well I got a critical man over here to work on." And they knew it, so I always had them wrapped around my finger. But every once in a while they lost their fucking cool and fucking started yelling. They forgot where they were.

But, anyway, the lieutenant colonel says, "Ventura, I want to thank you for saving my life."

I didn't tell him then I was trying to kill him. He might have pulled the same thing on me. I'll wait till we're out in the field. They gave me a medal. A Bronze Star. Big deal. A fucking fifteen cent piece of metal.

So anyway, he come over to me after the ceremony. And he says, "Tell me something, just between me and you. Were you really trying to kill me?"

I said, "Yah, I was trying to kill you."

He said, "Why?"

I said, "Why do you think?"

He says, "Sure I fuck with you once in a while, but I'm just doing it for your best interest."

I said, "My best interest? Every time I come out of the field, I got to work my ass off digging bunkers and filling sandbags? And you're looking out for my best interest? What the fuck am I going to do, take up a trade when I get back to the States filling sandbags? I'm sorry. I got no fucking use for that industry."

He says, "You don't have to be insubordinate about it."

I said, "Yeah, I was trying to blow your fucking head off. What did you think?" I said, "You think I love you or something?"

He said, "All right, Ventura."

So the next fucking day they had a ceremony and took back the medal. The NCO I got along with.

He says, "Come on, Ventura. They've got some kind of ceremony. The lieutenant told me to come get you." He says, "Oh yeah, bring that Bronze Star too. Pin it on over your lefthand pocket." So I pinned it on.

So they had this ceremony. And the battalion commander
gave me a big speech about "better men deserve this" and this
and that and all this bullshit. He didn't take it, he ripped it
off.

So I said, "Fuck you. Stick it up your ass."

He said, "I'm putting you in for a court martial."

I said, "Go ahead. How would you like me to tell your wife
that you've been going down to the village every night and
fucking some gook."

He says, "You can't prove that. Besides you don't know my
address."

I said, "I can find out easy enough from the mail clerk."

He says, "You wouldn't dare."

I said, "Push me, you'll find out."

So he goes to me, "All right Ventura, I'm not going to be
harsh about it. But I have to take this back anyway."

I said, "Fuck you." So he called me to attention. I had to
salute him. So I gave him a left hand salute. That means,
"Fuck you."

They fucking wave to you with one hand and throw a
grenade at you with the other hand. We were on a convoy
one time, I killed this kid six years old — he must have been
about six years old. And a couple of new guys in the company
used to shy away from me, maybe they thought I was nuts, or
because I'm a kid killer or some shit. But the kid was waving
to us and he pulled the pin on a grenade when the truck
passed by and threw it in the back of the truck. And this guy
fucking threw the grenade out of the truck just as it blew up.
And it blew his fucking whole arm off. I turned around and
shot the motherfucking kid.

What am I supposed to do, let the kid go unharmed because
he's six years old? Shit, them kids over there are not like
fucking kids over here. Kids over there they fucking grow up
quick because they're always around hostility and fucking

fighting and shooting. They know what's going on. They know if they get hit by a gun they're going to kill somebody, or they can get killed. They ain't stupid. So they can't fall back on that shit with me, 'cause if the motherfucker tries to shoot me, I'll shoot back.

And now it just got to the point when I got back to the States after spending the year over there, if he's going to shoot at me, I'm going to start aiming to kill. It's self-preservation. It's common sense. Maybe we're friends now. Maybe he might turn around one day and become jealous because I used to go out with her. And when my back's turned, blow my head off.

I blew up on the DA. 'Cause it just got me disgusted a fucking punk like that. Fought his way out of going to 'Nam, or the Army, and he's going to sit there and criticize somebody else. I don't know. I got real pissed off.

I seen it happen after I got back from 'Nam. I was thrown in the stockade in South Carolina, and out of two hundred and something prisoners, more than two-thirds of them were fucking veterans of Vietnam. And it just seems like the Army is fucking all the guys that come back from 'Nam. They get the shitty details, they get put on KP, they get restrictions. And yet these fucking kids just out of basic are fucking walking around with three-day passes, or a week's leave after basic and all this shit.

And I'm saying to myself, "This is what I fought for? Just to come back and be treated like a fucking animal?" So I just started acting like an animal. This is the way they want to treat me. Fuck them. I didn't show no respect for nobody that fucking didn't show me no respect.

But I didn't plan it that night to kill them. I was going to kidnap her and the kid. I wasn't going to harm them. Her father was always talking about how much money he had. I seen his bank book one day. He had a couple of thousand —

a couple of hundred thousand. I was only going to hit him for twenty. That's enough to draw — not to draw suspicion. I just wanted the money and get the fuck out of the country. I figured if I can get enough money to get out of the country and get stranded someplace in Europe or something, then whenever that urge came up to kill them or something, I'd be too far away. By the time I raised enough money to fucking get back to the States or something I'd be calmed down enough to say, "Fuck it." Then I'd go spend the money again before the mood comes on again.

After they had me locked up on them two charges, I had got out, and I started getting that urge again. So I took jobs with a truck driver going out west. He let me off in Denver, Colorado. I was there a couple of days and then the mood came on me again. Whenever I get in a mood where I'm frustrated, where I'm angered and I want to kill somebody or beat somebody up, I'll just sit down and I'll write a threatening letter or something. I'll put down on paper what's going through my mind. Then after I mail it I fucking say to myself, "Why the fuck did I go off and mail that motherfucking thing for?"

And this is what happened this one time I told them I had a .44 magnum pistol. And they had called the cops. They had a warrant out for me. About a week later I got into Auburn, I got picked up by the Auburn cops: "We got a warrant for your arrest in Corning," and all this shit. The Corning police came down, and they took me. I was writing threatening letters from the jail too.

And what letters Michelle got she sent to the police department. And the judge read them all, and he must have thought I was nuts or something. This was about three months after they were married.

This one time I had come to Buffalo, I had come looking for her. I was up in Connecticut with this buddy of mine I

was overseas with. And I had stayed with him a couple of
weeks. And the mood came on. And I stole his father-in-
law's car — an old beatup station wagon. And I just headed
for fucking New York.

So I came up to Buffalo on a bus. I was waiting for a bus.
And I got on the bus, and I was waiting, and I turned around.

And here was this girl who looked exactly like Michelle,
except her hair was a tinted blond and brown. And that's the
way Michelle used to wear her hair once in a while. And I
walked past her and she looked at me, but she didn't show no
sign of recognition. So I thought maybe she thought she was
seeing things too. You know, like it was her. So I followed
her on the bus, and I waited in the back, and she got off on the
city line.

And I waited 'til the bus was fifty, sixty feet past, and I rang
that thing, "Sorry, I uh, that was my stop. Let me off please."

The guy let me off. I doubled back, ran down the road up
behind her. And when I got close enough, I started walking
up near her.

And I called, "Michelle?"

And she turned around and she said, "Yeah, what?"

And I had the gun on her. And she half smiled. Then she
seen the gun. Then she grabbed her stomach, like I had shot
her, you know. And she smiled. And when she smiled, that
was the only thing that stopped me from shooting her. Because for everything else she looked like Michelle, except
Michelle had an extra tooth sort of that stuck out between this
tooth and this tooth. But this girl had all perfect teeth.

So I said, "Well I made a mistake. I thought you was
somebody else. I'm sorry."

Then I asked her where Union Road was. And she told me.
But she didn't put in no complaint. She just told the police
that I had a gun and that I was looking for somebody and I
was heading for Union Road. That's when I got picked up.

Whenever the pigs are chasing me for some reason or other, or someone's looking for me, I always become on the offensive side. I visualize them as the enemy. And I don't know about anybody else, but regardless of how small the gooks were, they put fear in me. And I knew I didn't want to be taken alive. So I'd always visualize this.

So whenever the cops were looking for me, if I ever got pursued, I'd rather die first then be taken alive. And this is the way I always thought. And the same thing with them. I was always on the alert. I would sleep with my eyes closed but my ears open. If I heard anything like a braking of a car, I'd open my eyes right away and look around. If there was a cop, I'd just fucking take off like a bat out of hell. I didn't care about the odds.

It seems funny. All the other times, the odds were against me whenever I tried to kill them or somebody. And yet all the ways up here the odds were with me, and it was remarkable. 'Cause for me, if it wasn't for bad luck, I wouldn't have any kind of luck at all. And yet the odds were with me all the way. I was surprised. At times I was disappointed. 'Cause I did things that normally other people would fucking get killed doing. I just started to do reckless things on purpose.

That morning I was being chased by a cop. The thought occurred to me, then I didn't go through with it, why don't I just turn the wheel around quick at this intersection and fuck everybody up — including myself? I can't miss. With the cop right behind me and there's traffic coming in both ways, I'm bound to get a fucking score or hit.

And then I said, "Fuck no. Why do that? What if the other guy doesn't get killed? Then I die and the motherfucker that's chasing me, he's still alive. And he gets credit and a medal and all this and a pat on the back."

Big deal. That's why I turned myself in. 'Cause I didn't want the credit to go to some fucking pig. Big hero. He killed — he caught the killer. Nobody caught me. If I wanted to get away with it, I would have got away with it. But I wasn't trying to get away with it.

So I went there to kidnap them. I got down at the end of the block and I was sitting there waiting. Then things started coming back to me from the 'Nam. Like the way you'd set up ambushes. You had to be quiet and you had to listen. Your eyes were nothing in the jungle at night. The only thing you had to keep open was your ears. Finally I figure I'd do it this way: I put on my coveralls — army fatigues, and my sneakers over my clothes. And I put mud or something on my face, because I knew the fucking grease from my nose and forehead would shine. If somebody had to see me out there, all they'd see is a fucking shadow. They wouldn't know what the shadow is, and nobody can come out there and investigate. But if they see something shiny, they might investigate or call the cops or some shit.

So anyway, I snuck up to the first fence and climbed over it. I didn't climb over it, got up to it and I just about fell over it. Then I was going across this bush, and these people were having a party or something. They threw on these floodlights. And this broad jumped over the bush, or pushed over this hedge, about five feet in front of me. She just got back up and climbed over the hedge and didn't see me. So I was crawling there with my gun. I had to go through four or five fences.

Then I snuck up to the house and looked around: nobody. So I went up the stairs. I knocked on the door. I had it all planned. If he didn't open the door up, I'd say "Police officer" or "Western Union" or some shit. But he opened the door. Then he closed it quickly. Then he opened it up again.

And he says to me, "Now Chopper, you don't want to do this. You don't want to spend any time in prison," and all this.

And I'm saying, "What are you talking about?"

He says, "The police already told us that you were going to come here to kill us. And we didn't think you would. We thought that was just another scare or something."

I said, "Kill you? I didn't come here to kill you."

"Then what are you doing here with a gun?"

I said, "I'm going to take Michelle and Mikey and you for ransom."

He says, "You're kidding."

I said, "No. Does it look like I'm kidding?"

And he said, "Anyway, come on in." I started to walk in.

Then it dawned on me.

I says, "He's letting me in awful easy." Whenever something comes too easy for me right away I'm suspicious.

I says, "Who's behind the door?"

He said, "Nobody."

I look behind the door, the crack of the door, and he went for the fucking gun. So I was wrestling with the fucking gun with him. Finally, I kicked him in the stomach and pushed him back against the wall.

And then I heard the people downstairs come upstairs talking. And I don't know, she came out and I didn't see her then, but he was half dressed. I don't know. I can't explain it. All kinds of things were rushing through my head at one time. And everything was kind of hazy like. You know, dazed and everything. I don't know how to fucking say it. I can't express the feeling. But everything was slow and hazy.

And I remember lifting up the gun and firing. You see a flash and that's it; but this flash lasted longer than a gun flash should. And the pellets, they came out: some were red and some were black and some were yellow. It was weird. I could see them in a pad just hit his chest. And as they hit his chest, they went in, and something came out. And then he stood there waving like that. I didn't want to see him suffer, or something — I don't know why, but I shot him again in the neck. And then he fell down.

And then she came out.

And she says, "What did you do?" And she says, "No. Not me. Not me."

And he had gotten back up. He didn't get back up, but he was on his elbow or something.

He says, "Leave Mikey alone. You're not going to hurt Mikey."

I said, "No. I'm not going to hurt the kid."

I wasn't going to hurt anybody until that happened. All kinds of shit was going through my mind. I didn't see it, I felt it. I'm not saying like I seen it on a motion picture: scenes going by. I felt the thoughts. And that wasn't just in thinking about it. I felt them like a person who's blind can read Braille.

And he said, "Leave the kid alone." Then he passed out.

And that's when she came out. And I stepped over him. And she came out. And I just remember raising the gun to her and hitting her. She just floated like. It was like that commercial on TV with the Prell they used to have on. They dropped the pearl in the Prell and it just float down. It was like that. I hit her. And she wasn't going floating down there like a feather or something like that; I mean she was. Then I heard the sound, after she hit. It must have been a couple of seconds. Then the sounds started coming back to me: the explosions. It's like watching a movie, and seeing the picture first and then after the first scene goes by you hear the sound from the first scene. And this is what everything was like.

And all I remember was turning around and running. And I just ran, just like fucking cops were after me. There was no cops after me. I don't know, I just kept on hopping over fences. And I remember running and running and running. And I'm trying to run as hard as I can. And yet I felt like I was fucking going through fucking quicksand or something. I mean everything was flashing by fast enough, but I didn't feel like I was running fast. I don't know. It was all fucking mixed up. But anyway, I had gone through this yard and a cop — they didn't say nothing at the trial, but I had shot at them. I'm pretty sure I fired about four or five shots at them. 'Cause I remember reloading as I was going.

And I remember when the car was parked next to my car — some car. And I detoured and went in back of their car. Their car was to my back. And I went in back of their car and they turn around and come up the driveway. I thought they had seen me.

And I had turned around. I started opening up on them. I fired about three or four shots. They didn't even mention that. They said they turned around and they received a call that there's been some shooting, and they turned around to investigate it.

I remember even hearing them fucking say, "Halt or I'll shoot."

And all I remember is I started opening up on the motherfucker. And then I started thinking quick. I figured if I carry this gun and these clothes they're going to recognize me. So I got rid of the gun; I threw it down. I took off the clothes and I put them down. There was a pounding in my heart, like I was really scared and everything, you know.

And maybe an hour later or so, I was sitting in the backyard, I was thinking about it. It was exciting. I mean, I realized what I did. I mean I wasn't sure if they were dead or not. I guess at the time I was hoping they were. So I wouldn't have to go through that again. All that fucking shit. It was weird.

It's different in 'Nam when you kill somebody fifty or sixty feet away. But when you kill somebody that close up, or shoot somebody that close up, I don't know, they didn't make any contortions with their face or anything, but it was, I don't know, it was something, something unfair about it, you know. It was like I stole their lives. I didn't take them; I stole them. I had the right to do it, but I didn't have the right to do it that way. At least call them up and tell them, "I'm going to kill you." Let them be prepared or something. And I had taken their lives in foul play like.

But anyway, I ran around this house, and I jumped in this fucking five-ton, a dump truck I guess it was. And I jumped in and I laid there and I was breathing heavy and everything. I remember catching a glimpse of two people out of the corner of my eye. And I was listening. I had my ears open again listening for sounds: footsteps, cars, or anything, yelling and screaming. And I picked up distant screamings or yellings or something. I rested a little bit more and I jumped out of the truck and I started running.

I went through jungles. I went through a yard. I jumped over the yard and I was in shoulder-high grass — bushes, or something. I remember running through that. And I remember hearing the squish and squash, like suction of mud when you step in mud.

And then I remember hearing all kinds of noises around me. Not crickets or anything. I remember hearing, I don't know, not jungle sounds. I mean they were mixed. There was — I don't know. I can't explain it. There was all kinds of noises, that I was familiar with, yet I wasn't familiar with. I could remember what they were, but I couldn't place them — where I'd heard them. I've been in the woods before and I slept in the woods before, but these sounds weren't like that. They were like, I don't know, I can't explain it.

Anyway, I was running and then I came across a hole. I fell in a hole or something, I don't know what it was. I thought it was a trap. Something bit me. I don't know what the fuck it was, but something bit me. I jumped out of the hole. I thought it was a snake or something.

And I started running again, and I remember running and running and everything. I got that feeling again that everything was passing me by fast. But yet I didn't feel it. I didn't feel as though I was running fast.

And then the noise blanked out. And I remember going through a fucking riverbed or something, 'cause the water was up to my knees. And I know it was water. I mean it was wet. I don't know if it was water. And I just kept on going and going, going. I don't know, I must have went through a mile of it — half a mile of it. There was a lot of riverbeds like that in Vietnam. Not really beds. They call them streams or so.

It was at nighttime. I wasn't even aware of sight. All I remember is just running straight ahead and staring. That's all. I wasn't even aware of what was around me, 'cause it was dark and my eyes are bad anyway. So anyway I had been running. And then I remember going up, I'll say a riverbank. I don't know if it was a riverbank. I remember going up a hill or something. And it was all crowded with fucking tall grass and bushes and everything.

And I had reached out and grabbed on to something, 'cause I started to slide. And it was a snake. I know this was a snake, 'cause the thing wrapped around my hand. Quick I took it off. I was thinking of the fucking viper snakes over in 'Nam. When I felt this I said, "Oh, shit." And it made me run faster or something. I just kept on going. And finally I went through yards and houses. I ran through one yard with people were having a picnic or something. They seen me, and I just went over the fence.

And finally, I don't know how far away I was, I just said, "Fuck it." I just got out on the sidewalk and started walking.

I said, "Fuck it. Why am I running for?" It just dawned on me. Why should I fucking run? I succeeded in what I was wishing all along. And it really happened. Whether they were dead or not, I'm not sure. Because I remember hearing a siren, and I didn't know. Later when I was recollecting my thoughts I was thinking maybe they ain't dead. Maybe they're just critically injured or something. Then I got depressed when I heard that. I said, "Oh fuck. All this shit and they ain't dead." I don't know. It was all mixed emotions. At the time I was glad. And I didn't care.

I said, "Fuck it." I wrote the judge and told him, "Yeah. I'm guilty. Send me away. I don't give a fuck. Just don't be fucking with me."

Sometimes during that night I decided to turn myself in. And then I'd stop, and said, "No. What am I doing? I'm fucking not going back into a cage again. They'll lock me up." I wouldn't care if they shot me, but I want something to fight back with. I'm not just going to say, "Here I am" and get blown away.

If I had a gun in my hand, I'd — just something I don't know what it is. If I died it wouldn't bother me as long as I had a gun in my hand and I took somebody with me. Dying alone — it had an eerie thought on me. It's just like maybe that's why I felt the same way about these people, 'cause they died without even having really a chance to fight. Even though they'd been fighting me for two and a half years, having me locked up and put in mental institutions and everything else.

I don't know, I wanted to die, but I wanted to die, this might sound silly, because to me I never thought of anything as honor, but I wanted to die honorably, you know. I wanted to die knowing that the guy that killed me isn't alive to fucking brag about it. 'Cause he's dead too. This is the way I felt. And sometimes during the night I wanted to turn myself in. Then I'd catch myself. "What am I doing turning myself in? These people don't give a fuck about me."

And then in the end I wound up turning myself in anyway, because Herb [his lawyer] wanted me to so we could beat it.

But I said to myself, "Look, I didn't call him because I wanted a lawyer. I called him because I wanted to get four bucks off of him. I had told him that I wanted it for a bus ticket to Auburn. What the fuck am I going to use with a bus ticket to Auburn? I wanted the money to buy some sleeping pills — fifteen sleeping pills. They cost three fifty or four dollars. I was going to kill myself. It's better than fucking rotting in prison. I don't know how courts can think they're being merciful by giving you life imprisonment. What's so merciful about that? I'd rather get the elec — I mean the electric chair ain't no big thing to jump and joy about. I could think of better ways of dying. But at least it's over with.

I didn't want to kill nobody else and I didn't want to turn myself in, at the same time. I was mixed up. Picture yourself in the middle of a tug-of-war and you're in the middle of it. You're the fucking post. And you can't decide — okay, say it was up to you, you can't decide whether you want to fall on that side of the line or this side of the line. So you just stand there like a fucking stone. You don't know which way to move.

And a lot of times this — this has happened to me a lot of times, in 'Nam it happened to me a lot of times. Like one time, this lieutenant — I liked him, he was O.K. But he did something to me — well, to somebody, a friend of mine, and I didn't like it. I had the urge to kill him. But I couldn't bring myself to kill him because I think about things he did do. And it just seemed like a change. And in this minute of indecision, the decision was made up for me; somebody else shot him. A lot of things like that.

There was a time after it happened where a cop car was coming down the road, and I didn't want to run. I was going to stand and fight.

I just walked right up to the guy and I asked him, I says, "How do I get to French and Union Road?"

I was kind of dazed. A lot of things were going through my head. I had read the paper the next morning: "COUPLE SHOT." I read it, and a lot of things were going through my mind. The guy had a picture of me on his seat. And I realized then — it came back to me where I was and what happened. If he would've went for his gun, I think I would've just gouged his eyes out. But he didn't. He just said, "Two blocks up that way and go to the right."

I bought the newspaper from a kid. Everything was like a bad dream. 'Cause all night I was experiencing the same thing. Going over and over again the whole thing. It was like seeing a rerun of a movie again.

And I bought this paper, and there it was on the front page, and I read it. I don't know what I wanted to do. I called him and he wasn't home. So I just walked into this open field, a school field, and I was walking around. I just kept reading the article over and over again. I don't know. There was something unreal about it when it happened. I thought maybe it was just something to smoke me out. You know, maybe they were just saying this to bring me out in the open. Maybe they weren't dead.

And I decided to walk up this road. And this dog came up to me, then just started barking and growling at me.

The guy, the owner of the dog told me, "That's unusual. I've had him for four years, that's the first time I've ever seen him growl at somebody like that."

I was joking with the guy; well, he thought I was joking anyway.

I said, "Maybe he smells death on me." I was serious.

The guy started laughing. He said, "Yeah, maybe he does."

But then I went down to the 'phone and I called him. That's when I asked for the money. He says, he can't do that. I said, "Nobody's got to know about it." So then he talked me into it.

I said, "No. I don't want to." I started crying. Because I remembered what happened in jail.

And he says, "Look. Wait for me."

I told him where I was.

"I'll bring somebody down, so they don't just start shooting at you."

I said, "Well I don't care about that."

He wanted to know if I had the gun. I didn't have it.

But I said, "Even if I did have it, I would have said, 'No.' " Why aid the enemy and let them know what kind of fire power I got?

Even when I came up they were cautious. They didn't have the guns out, but they were ready to grab them. 'Cause they had their coats open over the holsters. But I was sitting there on this bridge across from the gas station.

When I made the 'phone call, I was calling and this lady in this gas station was reading the paper.

And she says, "Ain't that a shame. Some nut running around killing innocent people."

I said, "How do you know the people are innocent?"

She looked up at me. I don't know if she guessed it or what, but she shut up after that. As if I knew too much, like maybe she thought I knew too much for her to say something like that. Maybe she figured out: maybe I didn't read the paper article. How the hell does she know what I'm talking about? Anyway, I don't know what it was, but she didn't say nothing after that.

So I went across the street to this bridge. This bridge, it was closed down because it was unstable. And I was standing up there, and I was thinking to myself, "If I had the gun, this would be a beautiful fucking OP [observation post]." 'Cause I could just sit right up there, and there's only one main road they'd have to come by. And I could just have a fucking target practice. And I was sorry I dropped the gun then. Like

I said, I didn't mind dying, I just wanted to take somebody
with me.

And then two cars went by, and I knew they found the gun
then. Two cop cars went by with their sirens going down
French. They came down Union, then they turned down
French. Then I kind of just walked out dazedly. And Herb
pulled up with the two Buffalo detectives. They stayed a good
distance away, and let him talk to me.

If I had my gun there — I still had about maybe fifty
rounds — I think I would have sat right up there in the open.
Because in order for them to take a shot at me, they'd have to
stick their fucking head up. And I'd blow their fucking head
right off. And when I got down to five or six rounds left, I'd
just charge, while I was pumping. That's what I wanted to do.

I was thinking about it after I got up on top of there: "Well,
this would be a hell of a place to make a last stand." 'Cause
there was only one way they could come at me. That's what I
would have done. But I had no gun. I was going to pick up a
stick and make believe. I had some firecrackers in my pocket.
I was going to make believe I had a .22 or something, and set
off a couple of firecrackers, and make believe I was firing a
gun: the twig, you know, the stick. And just start charging.
By the time they realized I had no fucking gun — it was just
a branch, I'd be fucking dead.

But then that instinct came in again. "Why should I fucking
die, while that motherfucker that killed me is still alive." It
doesn't make sense to me. I don't mind dying, but like I said,
I want to take somebody with me. I want to take the guy that
kills me with me. That would be the hell of a thing wouldn't it?

Like you see in all these movies. All the good guys always
kill the bad guys. They walk on: the lone star and all this shit.
For once I'd like to change history and just fucking take the
good guy with me. The bad guys always get fucked up at the
end: violent death. Where the good guys, whenever they get

shot it's always on the ground, or it's always in a chair where they just slump over peaceably.

And I always think to myself: Why is it whenever they make fucking movies the good guy always has to die so nice and peaceful, and yet the bad guy always dies violently? Bonnie and Clyde died violently and they didn't die violently. I mean to me that wasn't violently. Violently means to me something where they were pumped full of lead while they were dying or they got their head cut off or amputated or they bled to death by amputation or something. That's what I would consider violently.

When I die, that's why I always want to charge. 'Cause I know a charging man, I learnt from 'Nam, a charging man is more feared. 'Cause you want to bring him down quick before he gets to you. 'Cause even if he runs out of ammunition, he can still ram your head with the fucking butt end of a gun. And so you want to cut him down before he gets near you.

So this is why I always think to myself: I'll run quickly and fast and screaming and everything, so that when I do I won't have to fake the screaming. 'Cause it just comes out of me anyway. I figure I'll scream and make them think I'm mad so that they have to blow my head off and make it as peace — as painless as possible.

And so I always look at it. Like guys in 'Nam, how they died: some of them would suffer for two or three hours and maybe an arm ripped off or a lung busted open or their guts hanging out. Seeing it so much, I don't know how the infantrymen fix their mind to it. But a medic is different. Well, this medic was different. Whenever I seen this happen I didn't just see it, I felt the pain that the guy was feeling. And I felt it so many times, that most people become numbed by it. I couldn't get myself to become numbed by it. Just thinking about it, I could feel the similar pains that the guy's feeling, even if I'm not working on him. It wouldn't make me throw up or anything, or turn my head away or anything. But I could feel the pain. I couldn't ignore the pain. And when the guy screams I can feel that scream emerging in my own throat. Every once in a while I just see things like this and I just let out a yell, and it makes me feel better. And this is why whenever I die I want to die that way — fast. I don't even want to notice it happening. With my fucking luck I'd probably wind up dying violently anyway, no matter how hard I try.

After I had gotten back to my senses, I went on the defensive. After all the actions, I just stopped; sat down in somebody's backyard. I don't know whose it was, and I just sat there. Then this cop came. And I just sat there and I was thinking about just yelling out and I'll hit him with a stone or something and have him shoot at me. But then I was thinking, then that thought came into my mind: What if he didn't kill me; what if I just fucking hit me in the leg or in the stomach or something? Fuck that. So I took off across the street and hid underneath some kids' pool.

It was exciting in Vietnam. 'Cause you always knew that sooner or later a stray bullet might catch you, your gun might jam on you, or anything could happen. Any freak accident could happen. Danger was always an excitement. I was accomplishing something by killing somebody where the odds were even steven. I could get killed just as easily as I kill him. And the odds — it was something exciting in the danger of it.

And when I got back from 'Nam everything was so dull. Like before I used to get excited just from watching a crack-up at Watkins Glen. And they didn't effect me no more. I just sit there. Big deal.

And I always had these dreams now that I wanted to get even with the law. Because the law protected them [the police] yet they were out to punish me. It looked just like they were against me, you know. Against me. Fuck everybody else. Just me. And I just wanted to get me a rifle some-where and all the ammunition, an inexhaustible supply of ammunition, just sit up on top of a roof and shoot cops, not just anybody.

I like to play everything fair. Even when I get in one of these moods where I want to kill these pigs, I wouldn't do it. I wouldn't sit on top of a tower and start shooting them as they start breaking up from changing shifts. I'd call them and tell them. That's just the way I am. Even knowing that I'd be giving them the advantage of being on the lookout for me. That's just the way I am.

I always talk about I don't like to cheat somebody. But here I wound up cheating them 'cause of the way I did it — the way I killed them. I wasn't going there to kill them. The intentions at the time was just to kidnap them. And the way I killed them wasn't fair. What they were doing to me wasn't fair either. But to me two rights don't make a wrong — I mean, two wrongs don't make a right. It didn't make sense to me the way I did it. I felt guilty about it. Not for killing them. I didn't care that I killed them. Matter of fact, I was glad. It was like a big load was lifted off my shoulders after so many years.

But it was just the idea of the way I did it that I felt guilty. I didn't feel guilty about killing them. It didn't bother me; it had no effect either way. Later on it did. I felt sorry for her. 'Cause I got in one of them moods where I did love her. And at the time I didn't feel guilty about it or nothing. 'Cause to me they got what they deserved. Matter of fact, it was more merciful what I did to them then what they did to me over two years. And this is the way I looked at it. And the way I did it was the unfair part. I cheated. I like to play everything fair.

I felt as if I was more of a man. 'Cause all along before then, I used to cower back. And just having a gun in my hand gave me a sense of power that with this gun I could play God.

I didn't have to just sit back and take abuse from people and all that bullshit. In 'Nam, there was no law. I mean there was laws, but you didn't pay attention to them. 'Cause you knew when it came right down to it you were on equal terms with everyone. There was nobody that had odds against you. 'Cause everybody had a gun, and everybody had a right to kill. And if somebody shot me, I know before I went down, I'd empty the magazine at him. I don't know if I'd hit him, but I'd die trying.

And when I got back to the States it was so unreal. 'Cause whereas over in 'Nam you always carried a gun with you to defend yourself, in the States you had to settle for second best with the cops. And if they didn't do nothing, then you're on your own terms. But you'd be found wrong no matter what they are. I couldn't understand that. It didn't make sense.

Why do you have the right to kill at war and not in the States? That wouldn't make sense at all. I mean, why? Because we're supposed to be civilized? Shit! Them people are just as civilized as we are, except their ways of life are different. It boils down to that. I mean, I didn't love them, but I didn't hate them either. I was just on neutral terms.

When I first started using a gun over there, it was like someone saying to me, "We're here. This is your right to fucking do whatever you want, whatever you think is right." 'Cause all my life I was always being on the receiving end of abuse and everything. And here I was given the chance to fucking make up my own mind. Like who's got the right to live and who's got the right to die. And there was a lot of times it came down to the point where people on my own side deserved the right to die for the things they do. Maybe I was being self-righteous. But I was looking at it from my point of view. 'Cause I was always on the receiving end. And I guess only a person on the receiving end would understand what it's like —

who really has the right to live or die. I mean, a person who never got fucked up or beat up by a brother or sister, or picked on because he was small or the smaller guy, wouldn't understand that. They'd think you were fucking nuts or you don't know what you're fucking talking about. But a guy that's on the receiving end all his life, he knows what the hell he's talking about. He knows who the bullies are and who deserves the right to go on living. That's the way I always looked at it. So when I got that gun, it was just like saying, "Well here, use your own judgment."

So when I came back from 'Nam, this was the way I was too. I mean I never carried a gun with me, but I always fought back. Then every once in a while, I'd get into one of these moods where I was scared. I don't know why I was scared, but I was scared. I was afraid to say anything to anybody, and that I'd get beat up so much or pushed around so much that I'd blow up and I'd be back in my old self again. "Fuck you motherfucker. Beat me up. I'll get you one of these days."

And that's the way it's been. Even now, certain people I remember now, if I'm in jail and I write and they never write back. Yet all along they're supposed to be my friends. My so-called friends. But now that I'm in jail and facing murder, they know the outcome is going to be guilty and sent to prison for life, they sit back and they say, "Well, fuck you. Now we can tell you what we think of you." And I remember this and when I get out I'll take care of them. Maybe some of them I won't kill, but some of them I'll fuck up so bad they'll wish they were dead. I know they'll get me one of these days if I don't keep my eyes open.

I try to be nice. I try to understand people. But people don't understand me. So I try to shy away from violence. It seems silly. I don't care if the DA don't believe it or not. But

I try to avoid it. Sometimes it just gets to the point where I start biting my hands, and my fingers. Like I'll sit there and I'll try and forget it and I'll just chew right down on my thumb. I break the skin once in a while, biting so hard. It's calloused now.